"Men of Whom the World Was Not Worthy"

Heroes of Faith in Hebrews 11

By Rand Zuber

Truth
Publications

*Taking His hand,
helping each other home.*™

ISBN 10: 1-58427-331-3

ISBN 13: 978-158427-331-8

First Printing: 2011

Photos by Mike Willis; Maps by Kyle Pope.

Truth Publications, Inc.
CEI Bookstore
220 S. Marion St., Athens, AL 35611
855-492-6657
sales@truthpublications.com
www.truthbooks.com

Table of Contents

Foreword

This class book is written to be used primarily in adult Bible classes, although it also would make a good Old Testament reference book. It attempts to introduce many of the Old Testament heroes, by not only studying their contributions to God's plan, but endeavoring to relate historical events, peoples, and other kingdoms of the world that were contemporary and touched their lives. The secular history is related in part in order to give external evidences to the historical accuracy of the biblical record. Many of the dates of the Bible characters, especially before the flood, are not known precisely and are approximate unless stated otherwise.

In preparing the chronologies, an attempt has been made to rely on the biblical dates primarily; however, when secular dates are known, those are used to confirm the periods of the Bible characters. Most secular historians do not accept that there was a worldwide flood in the days of Noah. This premise makes the task of constructing a chronology difficult at times. Also, the Old Testament used Aramaic or Hebrew names for many of the peoples and cities so it is difficult at times for one to relate those names with the mostly Greek names found in secular literature.

Having laid out the problems, it is very enlightening to know that the pyramids in Egypt may have been built over 500 years before Abraham was born. It is also helpful to know that the city of Ur, from which Abraham was called by God, was one of the most advanced and modern cities of the time. Thus, Abraham was called by God out of an environment of idolatry, ease, and beautiful accommodations to become a tent dweller and wanderer in a land not his own for the rest of his life.

After a study of this work, it is hoped that one can better appreciate the Biblical heroes' relationships to Jehovah God by knowing the events in the world that surrounded and influenced them.

The eleventh chapter of Hebrews serves as an outline for this series of lessons. The lessons are not separated into class periods but by topic. In the outline, as in the text of the lessons, the names of those men who are found in the lineage of Christ are written in **bold letters**. Read Hebrews 11 to briefly meet the main characters studied later in greater detail. Truly these were the great heroes of faith before the coming of our Lord Jesus, and as found in verse 38, they were "men of whom the world was not worthy."

Outline of Heroes of Faith
Based on Hebrews 11

The foreword, introduction, creation, and the world's first family is presented.

By faith Abel and **Enoch** gained God's approval. **Seth** was born.

By faith **Noah**, being warned of God, in reverence prepared an ark for the salvation of his household by which he condemned the world.

By faith **Abraham**, when he was called, obeyed and lived as an alien in the land of promise.

By faith **Isaac** was able to bless his children about things to come, and **Jacob** blessed the sons of Joseph and worshiped.

By faith Joseph, when he was dying, spoke of the exodus.

By faith Moses chose to endure ill treatment with the people of God rather than the passing pleasure of sin and led God's people through the Red Sea.

By faith Joshua obeyed God, and the walls of Jericho fell down. By faith **Rahab** did not perish because she welcomed the spies in peace.

By faith Gideon, Barak, Jephthah, and Samson conquered kingdoms and rescued Israel from oppression.

By faith Samuel dedicated his life to God who was with him and let none of his words fail.

By faith **David** conquered kingdoms and performed acts of righteousness.

"And all of these, having obtained a good testimony through faith, did not receive the promise, God having provided something better for us, that they should not be made perfect apart from us" (Heb. 11:39).

Introduction to Time before the Flood

Plan

The first two lessons concentrate on the main heroes of the Old Testament before the flood and attempt to understand who they were and what were their strengths and weaknesses. Later lessons will show what historical circumstances might have shaped the Bible's heroes and what was happening in the world around them. Professor Andre Parrot, the world famous French archeologist, has said: "How can we understand the Word, unless we see it in its proper chronological, historical, and geographic setting?"

The following is a portion of a sermon written in Marshall, Texas on June 4, 1944 by this author's grandfather, M. C. Cuthbertson, who was at that time the preacher at the church of Christ in Marshall, TX.

History is a great blessing to the world, for it gives us a real foundation for our own life. Through history, we live with those who have gone on, and are permitted to use from their experiences, many facts and lessons, which enable us to enjoy blessings and avoid dangers, that would not be ours otherwise. History is of two kinds: human and inspired. There are many of the human, but only one of the inspired,

the Bible. "Men spoke from God," so Peter declared in 2 Peter 1:21 and inspired history is the result. History is a narration of facts and events arranged in order, with their causes and effects. The Bible perfectly meets those conditions, in the field of inspiration. And through inspiration, God has given us a history of all that we need to know to be saved here and in eternity. The Bible is a history, inspired by God, of man, God, Christ, the Holy Spirit, and judgments of God. They, the inspired Scriptures, are to guide us into all things.

Paul gives us an example of the use of Scripture in Romans 15:4, "For whatsoever things were written in earlier times were written for our instruction, that through perseverance and the encouragement of the Scriptures we might have hope."

These remarks are apropos to this lesson and help to explain why it is good to study the Old Testament and examine inspired history as compared to secular history. In this lesson and in all of the following lessons whenever secular and inspired history do not match, then deference is given to inspired history with the belief that archaeology and secular history will eventually

find evidence which will agree with the biblical account.

Modern archaeologists, even in Israel, are casting doubt on using the Bible as a roadmap to history as appeared in an article in the *Smithsonian*, May, 2006 entitled, "Shifting Ground in the Holy Land." Although Haifa University archaeologist, Adam Zertal, is seeking ruins to corroborate what is written in the Bible, biblical minimalists argue that the Old Testament is literary rather than historical. They consider the Old Testament the work of ideologues who wrote between the fifth and second centuries BC and that Moses, Joshua, **David**, and **Solomon** never even existed. Some archaeologists once did not think the nation of the Philistines existed, but they now have found the evidence to show they did. Christians must have faith that the Bible is inspired and that God would not record myths or tell about people who did not exist. This type of lesson, which in part gives external evidence of the accuracy of the Bible, is greatly helpful in preserving one's faith.

Hopefully, one will also recognize that it is enjoyable to look at some interesting facts about the ancient world. Do you know what the first city of the world was and who built it? Do you know why the Pharaoh of Egypt during the time of Joseph (a Jew) not only tolerated Joseph, but exalted him to second in command; while 200 years later another Pharaoh enslaved the Jews in Egypt? If you want to know the answers to questions like these and see how the events and peoples of the ancient world may have influenced biblical characters, then this series of lessons should be interesting and enlightening to you.

The Old Testament gives the history of God's people, who after the time of **Abraham's** forefather, Heber, were known as the Hebrews or the Israelites. Most of God's people today are of the Gentile world, and some of their forefathers in the flesh were nasty opponents of God. Christians today are fortunate that they can be the *spiritual sons and daughters* of **Abraham** and therefore be God's people by adoption.

The world's first faithful man will be presented shortly, but first consider a brief summary of **faith**, creation, and the family from which he came. These men about whom you will be studying understood that it was important to have **faith** in order to please God. Hebrews 11:6 states, "But without faith it is impossible to please Him: for he that cometh to God must believe that He is, and that He is a rewarder of them that diligently seek Him." Christians must show their faith by believing what the Bible tells about God, these great men of faith, and God's miracles. In Hebrews 11:3 one can read that it is "by *faith* we understand that the worlds were prepared by the word of God, so that what is seen was not made out of things which are visible." To really understand how important faith is in pleasing God and how great was the faith of these patriarchs, Christians are required to demonstrate their faith by believing the first three chapters of Genesis which tell how God created all things. What good is it to see the faith shown by these great men and women if one does not have *the faith they need* to believe in God's first miracle? Jesus in John 5:45-47 tells us that we will not be able to believe in Him if we do not believe the writings of Moses, "But if you do not believe his (Moses) writings, how will you believe My words."

Creation and the First Family
Genesis 1:26-3:24; Hebrews 11:1-6

Timeline: ca. 4500 BC?

Archaeological Finds: None

Points to Remember

- Faith is the assurance of things not seen, and it is by this faith that we understand that the worlds were formed by the word of God.

- Without faith it is impossible to please God (Heb. 11:6).

- **Adam's** sin brought death into the world.

- The first prophecy of Christ is found in Genesis 3.

- Abel was the world's first faithful man approved by God.

The Creation

In Genesis 1:26, God said, "Let Us make man in Our image, according to Our likeness; and let them rule . . . over all the earth. And God created man in His own image, in the image of God He created him; male and female created He them." This is the beginning of man's existence as recorded by Moses in the Bible.

According to *Nelson's Bible Dictionary*, **Adam** was given "spiritual, rational, emotional, and moral qualities" just as all mankind has been given. Thus **Adam** was given free will to choose between good and evil

and to contemplate the greatness of God. Now, mankind is not able to converse with God as **Adam** did in the beginning, but by reading the Bible one can understand God's plan.

One cannot know the exact date when God created all things; but by using what we learn from God's word, we can know that God created the world by His word, and it was in the five days before He created man. It was not by some gradual process of evolution. In Exodus 20:11, it is stated, "For in six days the Lord made the heavens and the earth, the sea, and all that is in them, and rested on the seventh day; therefore the Lord blessed the Sabbath day and made it holy." Is there any scientific proof that what Moses said in Genesis and Exodus about the creation is true? No. As there was no human in the universe until **Adam** was created, the beginning truly cannot be scientifically studied or confirmed by the scientific method. But, as the writer of Hebrews states, it is by **faith** we understand that God made the worlds and mankind (Heb. 11:3).

The Biblical history of mankind begins in the Garden of Eden. It was somewhere in the Fertile Crescent of the Middle

East. In Genesis 2:10-14, Moses relates, "Now a river flowed out of Eden to water the garden; and from there it divided and became four rivers. . . .And the name of the third river is Tigris; it flows east of Assyria. And the fourth river is the Euphrates." This naming of the rivers established the general area to be what is now known as the Fertile Crescent.

It was a geographical area that started from Egypt and progressed through what was later known as the Promised Land (Israel) to Mesopotamia (the land between the Tigris and Euphrates Rivers). It was the center of civilization down to the Grecian Empire. This area has been called the "Cradle of Civilization." It was also the area where Noah and his family came from the ark to settle. With this geography in mind, let us begin our journey with **Adam,** as found in Genesis chapters 1-4.

Adam, meaning "red, ground," was the very first human on the earth that God created; and although he is not one of the heroes, it is fitting that we should consider the first man who was the father of the first hero, Abel. **Adam** and his wife called **Eve**, "the mother of all living things," were privileged to live in the most perfect place on earth—the Garden of Eden. Every tree that is pleasing to the eye and good for food was there along with the tree of life and the tree of the knowledge of good and evil. All they had to do was minimally cultivate the garden. They did not even have to water the garden because a mist arose from the earth to water the whole surface. At that time God gave them one rule, "You shall not eat from it (the tree of knowledge of good and evil) or touch it, lest you die." As we know, Satan (in the form of a serpent) tempted **Eve** to eat of it; and she and **Adam** sinned and brought sin into the world. God meted out severe punishments to all concerned:

To the serpent, God cursed him and caused all serpents to crawl on their bellies.

For Satan, God predicted that the seed of woman would bruise his head, meaning a near fatal blow that would come from Christ. *(This is the first prophecy of the coming of Christ, born of a virgin.)*

For **Eve**, God greatly magnified the pain of childbirth for her and subsequently for all women and put them in subjection to their husbands.

For **Adam**, God cursed the ground to bring forth weeds and thorns and caused the work to be toil for all men after that time. Physical death was introduced to the world.

God drove **Adam** and **Eve** from the Garden of Eden. The consequence of **Adam's** sin was spiritual death to him and physical death to all. The "last Adam," that is Christ, brought justification and eternal life (Rom. 5:14-19).

It is important to study the first prophecy of Jesus found in Genesis the third chapter where God is telling the serpent (Satan) his punishment for tempting Eve. In Genesis 3:14-15, we read, "And the Lord said to the serpent, 'Because you have done this, cursed are you more than all cattle, and more than every beast of the field; on your belly shall you go, and dust shall you eat all the days of your life; and I will put enmity between you and the woman, and between your seed and *her seed*; He shall bruise you on the head, and you shall bruise Him on the heel.'" **Yes, Satan urged the men of Jesus's time to crucify Him ("bruise His heel"),** **but Jesus would rise from the grave victorious over death and Satan ("bruise his head").** How can one understand and believe this prophecy from chapter three of Genesis and not believe what God said through Moses about the creation in chapters one and two?

So **Adam** and **Eve** were no longer able to live in the beautiful Garden of Eden? How long they lived there is not revealed. Since the mention of the Garden is short, one may think that it was a short time; but it could have been many years. Also, even though the Garden of Eden was near the Tigris and Euphrates Rivers, one cannot know where it actually was. When God expelled **Adam** and **Eve** from the garden, He did not want mankind to be able to find the tree of life. (To find how God kept humanity from finding it, read Genesis 3:23-24.)

So what can we say of **Adam**? Was he a faithful man? Do we find where he repented? Certainly he was not listed with the faithful worthies in Hebrews 11. We have to go to Abel before we find the first faithful man.

Questions

1. In what way is man created in God's image? _____

_____

2. When was the earth created, in relation to man's creation, according to the Bible? _____

_____

3. Where was the Garden of Eden? _____

4. Why can it not be found? _____

_____

"Men of Whom the World Was Not Worthy"

5. Name two of the rivers that flowed out of Eden to water the Garden? _____

_____

6. What does "Mesopotamia" mean? _____

_____

7. What was Satan's lie? _____

_____

8. What is the first prophecy about Christ, and where is it found? _____

_____

9. Why should we study the Old Testament and its characters? _____

_____

Assignment for Lesson 2

Read Hebrews 11:4; Genesis 4-5.

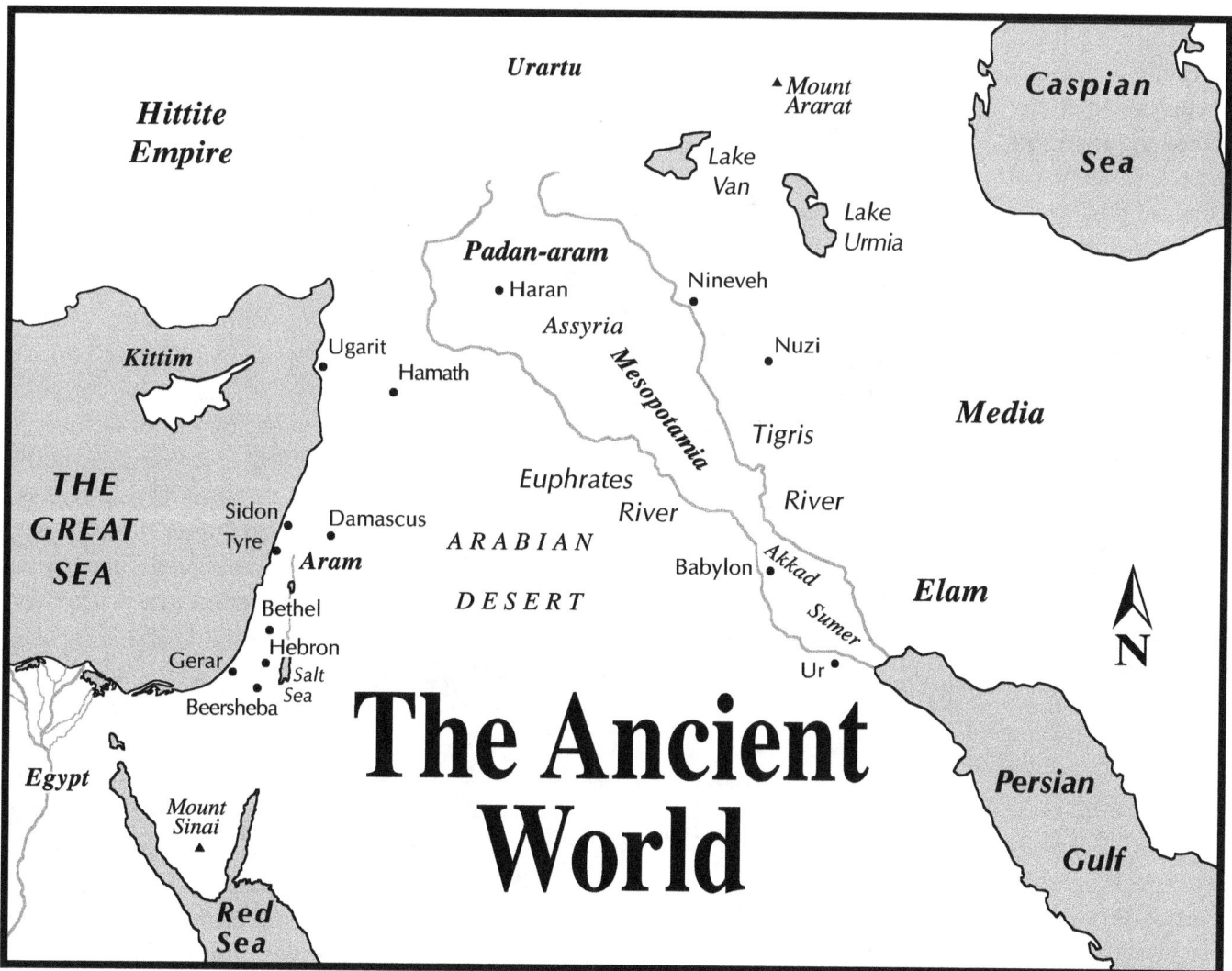

The Ancient World

2 Abel and Enoch
Hebrews 11:4; Genesis 4 And 5

Timeline: 4500-3000 BC?

Points to Remember: By faith Abel offered a better sacrifice to God than did Cain. In the days of **Seth** and his son **Enosh**, men began to call upon the name of the Lord. **Enoch** walked with God and he was not, for God took him.

Abel Was Killed

The world's first murder is recorded in Genesis 4:8. Cain, **Adam** and **Eve's** first-born, is described as a tiller of the ground; and his brother Abel was a keeper of flocks. Cain offered up a sacrifice that was displeasing to God because it was not based on faith. When his brother Abel's offering was accepted by God, Cain was jealous and killed Abel. It is interesting that it was Abel who is mentioned in Hebrews 11 as the first faithful man of the Old Testament. In Hebrews 11:4 we read, "By faith Abel offered to God a better sacrifice than Cain, through which he obtained the testimony that he was righteous, God testify-ing about his gifts, and through faith, though he is dead, he still speaks." How did Abel know how to offer the better sacrifice? Wasn't it by faith? In Romans 10:17 we read, "So faith comes by hearing and hearing by the word of God."

God evidently told Cain and Abel how and what to offer as a sacrifice. By offering a sacrifice pleasing to God, Abel offered a sacrifice of faith. We need to realize that man's faith is shown *by his works.* How does Abel still speak to us today? Are not Abel's works speaking to us as recorded in Genesis? Perhaps Abel is best known by the phrase, "He (by faith) offered a more excellent sacrifice than Cain."

Cain was "marked" because of his sin and sent off by God. He settled in Nod, east of Eden. We do not know exactly where Nod was. Remember that Moses, the author of Genesis by inspiration, was writing many years later about these events and sometimes called areas by what they were later known. [Consider Ur, referred to by Moses as Ur of the Chaldees. Ur at the time of **Abraham** was in Sumer (Shinar, in the Bible). The area was not known as Chaldea until hundreds of years later.] So Nod might have only become an area or town after there were enough of Cain's descendants to popu-late it. Where did Cain's wife come from? In the genealogies only some of the male children were named and almost none of the females. So Cain's wife was more than likely his sister or niece. We know that later the word of God forbade the marriage to a close relative (Lev. 18:6; 20:12). Perhaps one of the reasons is because in later generations genetic defects would be magnified by such unions. But in the beginning, God created us perfect without these defects. These defects could have gradually appeared after man was thrown out of the Garden and was exposed to the harmful effects of radiation from the sun, diseases, and the like. So, marriage between close kin was at first without harm and was needed to populate the earth.

Cain built the first city in the world, which was called Enoch after his first son. Other sons of Cain were Jabal, the father of tent dwellers; Jubal, the father of those who play the lyre and pipe; Tubal-Cain, the forger of bronze and iron, and Lamech. (Note: The Lamech who was the father of Noah, was not the same Lamech who was the descendant of Cain.) We see that bronze and iron came very early in man's history. When do the secular historians say that bronze and iron were first used? It is said that the Bronze Age started around 3500 BC. Unfortunately, all of Cain's living descendants died in the great flood of **Noah's** time.

After Abel died and Cain was banished, **Adam** and **Eve** had another son whom they named **Seth**. In Genesis 4:26, we read, "And to **Seth**, to him also there was born a son; and he called his name **Enosh**: then men began to call upon the name of the Lord."

The meaning of this passage seems to denote that **Seth** and/or his son **Enosh** began to pray to God. **Seth** became the son through which the lineage of Christ would come. He lived to be 912 years of age.

Another of **Seth's** later descendants was **Enoch** who did not taste of death because "he walked with God—And God took him." In Hebrews 11:5 one reads, "By faith **Enoch** was taken up so that he should not see death; *and he was not found because God took him up*; for he obtained the witness that before his being taken up he was pleasing to God." Other than Elijah, no other person was given such an honor. To walk with God and live faithfully all one's life should be the goal of everyone, but **Enoch** did it! **Enoch** was the father of **Methuselah,** the oldest man to live on the earth. He was 969 years old at the time of his death and probably died near or at the time of the flood. **Methuselah's** son was **Lamech,** the father of **Noah.**

So we find that Abel and **Enoch** were considered faithful enough to be included in the list of faithful heroes in Hebrews the eleventh chapter. Abel showed his faith by his sacrifice and **Enoch** was very faithful in his whole manner of life. **Enoch** walked with God for 365 years. We find it hard to be faithful for our meager threescore and ten. Is it any wonder that God found **Enoch** pleasing enough to keep him from seeing death?

Secular History before the Flood

There is not much known of secular history before the flood.

Either the art of writing was not in existence or it did not survive the flood. Most of what we know about the pre-flood peoples, other than what we find in the Bible, is in the buried remains of their pottery, carvings, weapons, or few permanent rock structures. What the people of **Noah's** time were like, what occupations they had, and what large cities existed are mostly lost to secular history. The Bible tells us that their thoughts were evil continually except for **Noah** and his family. The paleontologists would have us believe these people were for the most part cavemen types. Some, of course, probably lived in caves. Many peoples like the ancient Anasazi Indians of North America did; but most of the pre-flood peoples were intelligent like **Noah.** In Genesis 4, we learn that even as far back as Cain and his descendants, men were farmers, herdsmen, and practiced arts and crafts. Bronze and iron were used for weapons and implements. However, most of the descendants of **Adam** became extremely evil. God destroyed them, their culture, and the surface of the earth itself. We are left to pick up the secular history of civilization after the flood, somewhere around 3200-2500 BC. Secular history cannot be certain about how men interacted before the flood, or what their cities were like. We are, however, blessed with the inspired word that tells us what God wants us to know about the wickedness that grieved God so much He destroyed the world and all mankind except **Noah** and his family.

Questions

1. Why did Cain murder his brother Abel? _____

_____

2. Why did Cain ask God if he was his brother's keeper? _____

_____

3. Was he faithful? _____

4. Who does the writer of Hebrews list as the world's first faithful man? _____

_____

5. How do Abel and later the patriarchs speak to us today? _____

_____

6. Why did God allow marriage to close relatives in Old Testament times and not today? _____

_____

7. What was the first city in the world? _____

8. When did man first forge bronze and iron? _____

9. Who was the third son of **Adam**, and what does Hebrews 11 say about him? Was he faithful? _____

_____

10. Who was **Enoch** (son of **Jared**) and what is special about him? _____

_____

11. What do we know about secular history before the flood? _____

_____

Assignment for Lesson 3

Read Hebrews 11:7 and Genesis 6-11.

"Men of Whom the World Was Not Worthy"

Noah

Hebrews 11:7; Genesis 6:7-9:29

3

Timeline: 3700-2400 BC?

Points to Remember: The great flood of Noah's time was real and catastrophic to the earth. By faith, we can trace to the flood the fossil remains and the geologic layers found today. Noah and his family were the only righteous humans on the earth out of a population estimated to be in the millions. God gave us the rainbow as a sign that He would never again destroy the world by water.

Noah's Flood

The great flood of Noah's time was world wide and catastrophic. Peter tells us in 2 Peter 3:5-6, that the "world at that time was destroyed by water," not just the destruction of life. When was the Great Flood of **Noah**? We, of course, cannot be certain as to the time, but the great civilizations of Sumer and Egypt, according to secular history, had their first kings and writings about 3000 BC. From a few inhabitants to a great civilization would take at least a hundred years, so if secular history is right about the time of the rise of the civilizations above, then one could deduce that the flood was about 3100 BC. However, the secular 3000 BC date is estimated, and the Bible leaves the date unrevealed.

According to Alden Bass in "Which Came First, the Pyramids or the Flood?" the backbone of Egyptian chronology is the regnal lists, the most prominent of which is composed by Manetho, who was a priestly advisor to Ptolemy I (323-282 BC). This work tells of the kings of Egypt and gives the years of their reigns.

It appears that the first king, Menes (Aha) [1st dynasty], united the upper and lower kingdom of Egypt about 3000 BC; and the first pyramid was supposedly built about 2650 BC. However, there appear to be some errors since dates were calculated on astronomical dating and assumed no changes in the Egyptian calendar, though now there is in secular history "general" agreement on circa **3000 BC** as the start of the Egyptian civilization.

Some studies, as seen below, point to a global climate change which occurred about 3200 BC.

Based on studies by glaciologist Lonnie Thompson (professor at Ohio State University and researcher with the Byrd Polar Research Center), a number of indicators show there was a global change in climate 5200 years ago:

Terah is born	Sons are born (Gen. 11:26)		Abraham is born; Terah is 130	Terah dies at 205; Abraham is 75
		60 missing years		

- The climate was altered suddenly with severe impacts.

- Plants buried in the Quelccaya Cap in the Peruvian Andes demonstrate the climate had shifted suddenly and severely to capture the plants and preserve them till now.

- A man trapped in an Alpine glacier ("Otzi the Iceman") was frozen until his discovery in 1991.

- Record lowest levels of methane retrieved from ice cores from Greenland and Antarctica.

- End of the Neolithic Subpluvial, start of desertification of Sahara. North Africa shifts from a habitable region to a barren desert.

- Disastrous floods in Mesopotamian region.

Couldn't these changes have been caused by a world wide flood?

It is uncertain when the flood of **Noah's** time occurred. Josephus believed the flood was around 2350 BC. One can search for years and still be unable to find any consensus by biblical scholars on a date other than that the flood was about 1650-2262 AM (*Anno Mundi* – in the year of the world), in the years since the creation of the world, using strict biblical genealogy information.

The best date that fits secular history is circa 3200 BC, but the best date that conforms to the Masoretic text of the Bible is circa 2350 BC. Because Abraham lived approximately 350 years after the flood (Masoretic) and many believe he was born about 1951 BC, then according to the Masoretic text, the flood would have occurred around 2350 BC. The Septuagint's chronology conforms more to secular history and would date the flood nearer 3200 BC.

Biblical Dating of the Flood

Biblical scholars today are divided on which source to use to date the flood. We may never know for sure, but there are clues in the Bible. In 1 Kings 6:1 we read, "Now it came about in the *four hundred and eightieth year* after the sons of Israel came out of the land of Egypt, *in the first year of Solomon's reign* over Israel . . . that he began to build the House of the Lord." We know the year of the fourth year of Solomon's reign, to be 966-967 BC. If we add the 480 years back to the Exodus, we arrive at about 1446 BC. In Galatians 3:17, we read, "What I am saying is this: the law, which came 430 years later, does not invalidate a covenant previously ratified by God, so as to annul the promise." This is obviously the promise given to **Abraham** when he was 75 years old. So, adding 430 years to 1446 BC we get 1875-1876 BC as the date of the promise to **Abraham** (Beitzel). Adding the 75 years of his age to that date we get approximately 1951 BC as the birth date of **Abraham.**

Looking at the birth of **Abraham** from the flood forward we find that **Arpachshad** was born two years after the flood. Thus it was about 350 + 2 years after the flood (according to the Masoretic texts) that **Abraham** was born in the year 1951 BC.

This makes 1951 + 352 or 2303 BC as the year of the flood. This date is very hard to validate with secular history. Could there be gaps in the genealogies given in the biblical texts?

Again, quoting from Alden Bass, "Though various theories fall short, there must be a solution to the dating problem in the Bible. The flexibility of the Egyptian chronology has been demonstrated. What was once a thousand years difference in biblical and secular dates has shrunk to only about 250 years which can be found in the recesses of the biblical chronology. According to Genesis 11:26, Terah begat Abram, Nahor, and Haran in his 70th year. The boys were not triplets and other passages reveal that there were quite a few years between them. Terah had Abram when he was 130 years old. Thus we have clear evidence of the possible addition of a number of years from the flood to Abraham."

Similarly, Hoerth, when discussing pre-Abrahamic chronology says, "In the Ancient Near East it was common practice to use 'selective genealogies' when ordering history" (198). What did he mean? In Ezra 7:3, Azariah was said to be the son of Meraioth, but in 1 Chronicles 6:6-9, six generations are listed between these two names. Clearly the word "begat" sometimes means "ancestor of" rather than the immediate "father of."

Thus we see that, even if we consider the Septuagint dates to have been added by later writers, there appears enough flexibility in the Masoretic dates to have secular and biblical chronologies to arrive at a time for the flood of about 3000 BC. It is certain that the Flood came before the pyramids. Again quoting from Alden bass, "It is foolish to suppose that the pyramids could have survived the flood—an event so fierce that 'all the fountains of the deep {were} broken up, and the windows of heaven were opened,' (Genesis 7:11) – and that the civilization of Egypt 'picked up where it left off' before the deluge." Also, it is known that the first pyramid was built by an "Egyptian," not some one living in the area before the Egyptians. From Genesis 10, we find that one of Ham's sons was Mizraim, the father of the Egyptians. Mizraim being born after the flood demands the pyramids to be built after the flood; and if the first pyramid was built in 2650 BC, the flood was prior to that date by a hundred or more years.

The Faith of Noah

In Genesis 5:32, we read, "And **Noah** was five hundred years old, and Noah became the father of **Shem**, Ham, and Japeth. In Genesis 6:1-7 we read, "The Lord was sorry that He had made man upon the earth and He was grieved in His heart. So the Lord said, 'I will destroy man whom I have created from the face of the earth, both man and beast, creeping things and birds of the air, for I am sorry that I have made them.' But **Noah** found grace in the eyes of the Lord . . . **Noah** was a just man, perfect in his generations. Noah walked with God." As James reveals in Chapter 2:14-22, the Old Testament worthies showed their faith by their works.

In Genesis 5:32, we read, "And **Noah** was 500 years old when he became the father of **Shem**, Ham, and Japeth. It then took **Noah** about 100 years to build the ark. It had never rained or at least never rained enough to float such a large boat built on dry land. Consider the faith that **Noah** exhibited to work on that boat for 100 years, being ridiculed by all around him. Nevertheless **Noah** persisted and even preached repentance to all who would listen to him.

Noah built the ark to the exact specifications given him by God. By obeying God *exactly*, **Noah** gives us an example of how we should obey God today in all that we do, especially in worshipping Him. How large was the ark? Can you imagine a boat so large that 522 boxcars could fit into the ark? It was 450 ft. long, 75 ft. wide, and 45 ft. high (using 18 inches to the cubit) Thus it was one and a half times the length of a football field.

Secular History of a Worldwide Flood

Are there any secular records of the great flood of **Noah's** time?

It is interesting that Sumerian and Babylonian versions of the flood have survived, and in important ways parallel the biblical account. The Gilgamesh Epic, a fictional story about one of the earliest Sumerian kings circa 2700 BC, also contains an account of the flood. Remember that the Sumerians and Babylonians believed in many gods so the story is slanted toward their beliefs. Gilgamesh himself did exist although this is a fictional account of what actually happened.

The following are excerpts from "The Epic of Gilgamesh" Tablet XI, the story of the flood.

> Gilgamesh spoke to Utanapishtim, the Faraway [possibly a reference to **Noah**]:
>
> "I have been looking at you,
> But your appearance is not strange
>   —you are like me . . .
> My mind was resolved to fight with you,
> but instead my arm lies useless over you.
> Tell me, how is it you stand in the assembly of the gods,
>   And have found life!"
> Utanapishtim spoke to Gilgamesh saying,
>
> "I will reveal to you, Gilgamesh, a thing that is hidden,
> A secret of the gods I will tell you!
> Shuruppak, a city that you surely know,
> Situated on the banks of the Euphrates,
> That city was very old and there were gods inside it.
> The hearts of the Great Gods moved them to inflict the flood.
> Their Father Anu uttered the oath of secrecy,
> Valiant Enlil was their advisor,
> Ninurta [this may be a reference to Jehovah God]was their
> Chamberlain . . .

O man of Shuruppak, son of
Ubartutu:

Tear down the house and build a boat!
Abandon wealth and seek living
    beings!
Spurn possessions and keep alive
    living beings!
Make all living beings go up into the
    boat.
The boat that you are to build,
Its dimensions must measure equal
    to each other:
Its length must correspond to its width.
Roof it over like the Apsu.
I understood and spoke to my lord, Ea:
'My lord, thus is the command
    which you have uttered
I will heed and do it.'

Just as dawn began to glow
The land assembled around me—
The carpenter carried his hatchet,
The reed worker carried his flatten-
    ing stone,
The child carried the pitch,
The weak brought whatever else was
    needed.
On the fifth day I laid out her exterior.
It was a field in area,
its walls were each 10 times 12 cubits
    in height,
the sides of its top were of equal
    length, 10 times its cubits each.
I laid out its interior structure.
I provided it with six decks.
Three times 3,600 units of raw bitu-
    men I poured into the kiln,
Three times 3,600 units of pitch.
Shamash had set a stated time:
'Go inside the boat, seal the entry!'
That stated time had arrived.
I watched the appearance of the
    weather—
the weather was frightful to behold!
I entered into the boat and sealed the
    entry.
There arose on the horizon a dark
    cloud.
Forth went Ninurta and made the
    dikes overflow.
The land shattered like a pot.
All day long the south wind blew,

blowing fast, submerging the moun-
    tain with water,
overwhelming the people like an
    attack.
One could not see his fellow.
The gods were frightened by the flood.
The gods were cowering like dogs.
Ishtar shrieked like a woman in
    childbirth.
Six days and seven nights
came the wind and flood, the storm
    flattening the land.
When the seventh day arrived
The sea calmed. Fell still, the whirl-
    wind and flood stopped up.
I looked around all day long—quiet
    had set in
And all the humans had turned to clay.
On Mt. Nimush the boat lodged firm.
When a seventh day arrived
I sent forth a dove and released it.
The dove went off, but came back to me;
no perch was visible so it circled back
    to me.
I sent forth a swallow and released it.
The swallow went off, but came back
    to me.
I sent forth a raven and released it.
It eats, it scratches, it bobs, but does
    not circle back to me.
Then I sent out everything in all
    directions and sacrificed a sheep.
I offered incense in front of the
    mountain—ziggurat (*www.
    ancienttexts.org/library/mesopot-
    amian/gilgamesh/*).

Gilgamesh was a real king. The
Sumerian king list established
a Gilgamesh as fifth in line of
the First Dynasty of kingship of
Uruk following the great flood
recorded in the epic, placing
him approximately in the latter
half of the third millennium. He
was supposed to have reigned a
hundred and twenty-six years. He
was known as the builder of the
wall of Uruk, and his mother was
said to be the goddess Ninsun,
wife of a god named Lugalbanda,

who however was not his father.
His real father was, according
to the king list, a high priest of
Kullab, a district of Uruk, from
whom he derived his mortality"
(*Gilgamesh: A Verse Narrative* by
Herbert Mason, Signet, 1972).

So, we have a record of the
flood told by heathens in a fanciful
tale, but we see that there are some
similarities with the biblically
recorded account of the flood. In
fact, many civilizations give an account of a worldwide flood. Each
one is different, yet with enough
similarities to support the idea
that *a world wide flood did happen.*

Secular Evidence of the Flood

One might ask, "Aren't there any
scientists who believe in the flood
of **Noah's** time who can present
evidence of the flood?" The answer
is yes! Although most scientists
are committed to Darwinism and
reject the flood, there are some
who have an open mind to see the
evidence. Dr. Andrew Snelling
shows evidence of the flood in his
writings and states, "The scientific
evidence (*of the flood*), correctly
understood, is totally consistent
with the Biblical account" (*Cre-
ationwiki.org/Andrew_Snelling*).

Descendants of Noah

Because of **Noah's** faith and
obedience, the Bible says his three
sons (**Shem**, Ham, and Japeth),
their wives, and his wife were
saved by the water and the ark.
Thus, his sons became the fathers
of all the nations of the world.

Genesis 10 states that the sons
of Ham primarily settled in Africa and Canaan. Ham's sons were
Cush, Mizraim, Phut, and Canaan.

"Men of Whom the World Was Not Worthy"

The Descendants Of Noah

HAM *Southern Areas*
Mizraim (Egyptians, Philistines)
Cush (Ethiopians, Nimrod)
Canaan (Canaanites, Heth, Sidon)
Phut [*Put*] (Libyans)

JAPHETH *Northern Areas*
(*Indo-Europeans*)
Javan (Greeks)
Magog (Sythians)
Madai (Medes)
Tiras (Thracians)
Meshech (Cappodocians)
Gomer (Galatia)
Tharsus (Cilicia, Tarsus)
Cethimus (Cyprians)

SHEM *Middle areas*
Elam (Persians)
Asshur (Assyrians)
Arpachshad (Born 2 years after the
  flood) [**Shelah, Eber** (Hebrews)]
Aram [Uz (Syrians)]
Lud (Lidians)

Descendants from Noah to Abraham

Noah
Shem
Arpachshad
Shelah
Eber
Peleg
Reu
Serug
Nahor
Terah
Abraham

The descendants of Mizraim were the Egyptians. The descendants of Canaan were the Canaanites and Hittites. Descendants of Cush besides the Ethiopians include Nimrod the mighty one on earth who established the cities and kingdoms of Babylon, Erech (Uruk), Accad (Akkad), and Calneh in Shinar (Sumer); and the descendants of Phut were the Libyans. Nimrod also went forth and built Nineveh and Calah and Rezsen. Mizraim also beget Cashluhim (from which came the Philistines).

Who was Nimrod? Was he good or evil? Read Genesis 10:8-12. Does anyone in secular history fit with the character and deeds of Nimrod? He was the grandson of Ham and thus lived within three hundred years after the flood. There are ruins of an ancient city named Nimrud not far from the ruins of Nineveh which points to Nimrod. Gilgamesh of the previous flood story seems to fit chronologically and was the first great city builder of around 2700 BC. Secular history attributes the building of Uruk (Erech) to Gilgamesh; where the Bible attributes it to Nimrod.

These similarities lead many to believe that Gilgamesh was Nimrod (*Who was Nimrod?*, David P. Livingston, PhD., C.F. Keil, and F. Delitzsch, *Commentary on the Old Testament*, vol. 1 [Grand Rapids: Eerdmans Publishing, 1975 reprint]) He started his kingdom at Babylon (Gen. 10:8-11). According to Josephus he may have been responsible for the tower of Babel which was possibly a modification of a ziggurat. Josephus also identifies Nimrod with Gilgamesh whose epic tale we have alluded to previously because of its reference to the flood. The name Nimrod comes from a Hebrew verb *marad,* meaning "rebel." The question arises, "Was he good or bad?" He was probably not a follower of God as he was a descendant of Cush. However, since he was so powerful and started so many kingdoms, one would expect to find him in the secular ancient literature. Indeed, Gilgamesh fits the type of leader that Nimrod was. The Sumerians, Babylonians, Assyrians, and Hittites wrote about such a vile man who defied God.

Shem was the father of the Asians that included the Persians, Assyrians, Lydians, and Syrians. **Arphaxad** (Ara Kessed), his son, born two years after the flood, was the father of **Salah**. **Salah** beget **Eber** the father of **Peleg**, for in his days the earth was divided as told in Genesis 11:1-9. Another descendant of **Shem** was Aram, the father of Uz and the Arameans, later known as the Syrians who settled in Haran. The Elamites (Persians) and Lud (Lydians) were also descended from **Shem.** The descendants of Shem became known as the "Semitic peoples." It was the descendants of **Eber** who began to be called "Hebrews," and some settled in the city state of Ur.

In Genesis 10 we find that another of **Noah's** sons, Japheth (the forefather of the Europeans) had

Gomer (Galatia, Cimmerians, ancient Armenians), Magog (Sythians), Madai (Medes, Iranians), Javan (Greeks, Tarsus), Tubal (Anatolia, Spain, Portugal, and Italians), Meshech (Cappodocians, and the Sea Peoples), and Tiras (Cethimus, Cyprians, Thracians).

Ruins of Ur with its ziggurat.

After the flood mankind migrated east to Shinar, which is known in secular history as Sumer. One of the most famous cities near Sumer was Babel (Babylon). The area today is known as eastern Iraq. The early settlers of Babel tried to build a tower into heaven and God confounded their tongues so that they all began to speak different languages. At this point read Genesis 11:1-9. Here one can find how the descendants of **Noah's** sons were scattered over the known world at that time.

Sumer, the First Civilization

We will now study the Ancient Sumerians of Sumer (Shinar as it is called in the Bible). It was in Uruk (Erech) that the Sumerians developed cuneiform writing and in whose ruins we find the oldest written records on earth. Some of **Shem's** descendants through **Arphaxad** (**Abram,** etc.) were in Sumer although most Sumerians were not Semitic and probably descended from Cush (Ham). The city state named Kish, in Sumer, could be a variation of the name Cush. Sumer's history goes back

to around 3000 BC, and is synchronous with the development of ancient Egypt founded by the descendants of Ham's son, Mizraim. The Sumerians wrote in cuneiform on clay tablets as opposed to the Egyptians who introduced papyrus and wrote in hieroglyphics.

The Sumerians studied arithmetic based on the number 10, but they multiplied 10 by 6 to get the next unit 60 and so on. The Sumerians divided the circle into 360 degrees. From the Sumerians came the term "dozen" (1/5 of 60) and the division of the clock with 60 minutes. Their measure of weight was the mina, made up of 60 shekels—the same weight as a pound. They developed the first calendar which they adjusted to the moon (lunar calendar). There are pottery finds from Kish, Eridu, Ur, and Ubaid in Sumer which have been dated to before the flood by some.

Sumer, in what is now southeastern Iraq, was a collection of city states with Ur, Kish, Lagash, and Uruk, being the most prominent. In 2500 BC, Uruk was ruled by Gilgamesh, perhaps the first "king" and the subject of the first epic poetry that was studied earlier.

As we know, **Abram** was called out of Ur in Sumer around 2000 BC. Ur was destroyed just a few years later by the Elamites. It was rebuilt and became part of the kingdom of Isin, later the kingdom of Larsa, and finally incorporated into Babylonia.

Ur was still an important center even under Assyrian rule. Nebuchadnezzar rebuilt the ziggurat of Ur during his reign in the 6th century BC, and it still stands today.

After Babylonia came under the control of Persia, Ur began to decline and was forgotten by the 4th century BC. During its excavation in 1922-1934, many art treasures and cuneiform tablets were found; some dating back to around 2700 BC near when the first Egyptian pyramid was thought to be built. An example is the standard of Ur found in the royal cemetery by Sir Leonard Woolley and can be seen in the British Museum in London.

Sargon

Sargon the Great will be mentioned here as he was one of the great empire builders of Mesopotamia and ruled about 200 years before Abraham. A king of Kish in Sumer, Sargon I, began to conquer the surrounding city states in 2334 BC. In 2320 BC he invaded Lebanon and created the Akkadian Empire. Sargon thus became one the world's first emperors and the best known. The empire was named after his second capital city, Akkad, established in 2340 BC. Sargon adopted a new Semitic language, known as Akkadian, which spread through Mesopotamia (Chaldea).

Rule over the Near East

While it is unknown exactly how Sargon came to power, he soon attacked Uruk, where reigned Lugal-zage-si of Umma. Lugal-zage-si, with fifty governors under his command, was defeated, captured and brought to Kish "in a carcan" and exposed at Enlil's gate. Sargon then attacked and crushed Ur, Lagash, and Umma. He made a symbolic gesture, washing his hands in the "lower sea" (Persian Gulf), to show that he had conquered Sumer in its entirety.

Late period

A late Babylonian chronicle says:

In his old age, all lands revolted against him, and they besieged Akkad. But Sargon went forth to battle and defeated them; he knocked them over and destroyed their vast army. Later, Subartu in their might attacked, but they submitted to his arms, and Sargon settled their habitations, and he smote them grievously (King, L. W. *Chronicles Concerning Early Babylonian Kings*. London: Luzac and Co.,1907).

Sargon was succeeded by his sons, Rimush and Manishtushu.

Questions

1. What does the writer of Hebrews say of **Noah** in chapter 11:7? _____

_____

2. About how long did it take **Noah** to build the ark? _____

3. Why did God destroy the earth? _____

4. Will God again destroy the earth? _____ With water? _____

5. Why did God limit the years of mankind? _____

_____

   To how many years? _____

6. How large was the ark? _____

_____

7. How does God's command to build the ark and **Noah's** strict obedience help us today to know how to obey God? _____

_____

8. Of the animals, how many of each clean and unclean kind were to be saved? _____

9. What promise did God make to **Noah** and his sons after the flood and what was to be the sign of that promise? _____

_____

10. Name at least three nations that came from each of **Shem**, Ham, and Japheth. _____

_____

11. How did **Noah** show his faith? _____

_____

Assignment for Lesson 4

Read Genesis 11-25.

4

Abraham
Hebrews 11: 8-19; Genesis 11-25

Timeline: 1952-1776 BC

Points to Remember: Abraham is the father of the faithful. He was called by God out of Ur, one of the most civilized cities of the world in **Abraham's** time, to live the life of a nomad. **Abraham's** faith grew to such great heights that he was prepared to offer **Isaac,** his only son by **Sarah,** as a sacrifice to God. **Abraham** offered a tithe to Melchizedek, king of Salem, priest, and type of Christ.

Abraham's Ancestry

The ancestry of **Abraham** is as follows: **Shem** begat **Arphaxad, Arphaxad** begat **Salah, Salah** begat **Eber, Eber** begat **Peleg, Peleg** begat **Reu, Reu** beget **Serug, Serug** begat **Nahor, Nahor** begat **Terah,** and **Terah** begat **Abram,** Nahor, and Haran. Nahor and Haran, the father of Lot, were probably older than **Abram.** Terah also had a daughter, **Sarai,** by another wife who became **Abram's** wife (Gen. 20:12). Eber's (Heber) descendants became known as the Hebrews.

Abram lived in the city of Ur in Sumer which is in southern Mesopotamia, or what is known as Iraq today. It was an idolatrous city, but it was one of the most advanced cities on earth. The queen of Ur even had indoor plumbing and running water.

At the time of **Abram,** though still a great city, Ur's influence was beginning to wane. The city was made out of bricks of burnt mud and clay similar to the great temple to Nana the moon god's monument, the ziggurat. A similar ziggurat was in Babylon which suggests that the Tower of Babel was just an extended "ziggurat." The word "ziggurat" means in the native tongue something like "the seat of heaven and earth." So **Abram,** living in relative prosperity and civilization, was called by God to leave and live his subsequent life as a wanderer living in tents, in a land not his own. Perhaps, knowing the greatness and wealth of Ur, one can better see the great faith **Abram** had in obeying God and going to live the life of a wanderer in a strange land (Gen. 11:31-12:4) Today one can see only the ziggurat standing and the ruins of some of the walls of the city of Ur. Many valuable artifacts have been found there.

At first **Abram** went with his father to Haran near the city of Mari in what is now Syria, but was called Padan-Aram in Genesis 25:20. However, God told him to separate from his kindred and go into the land of Canaan. God established a covenant with **Abram** when he was 75 years old. God said He would make

of **Abram** a great nation and in **Abram's** seed should all families of the earth be blessed.

Abram's migration from Ur, according to the biblical chronology, took place in the region about Haran which was probably under the control of Mari.

The city of Nahor (Gen. 24:10) is mentioned quite frequently in the Mari letters (*www.theology. edu/httm*).

Abram or **Abraham** (father of a multitude of nations) as his name was changed to by God in Genesis 17:5 is known as a faithful man and even referred to as the "father of the faithful." However:

There were times when **Abraham's** faith was in the process of growing. When traveling to Egypt, **Abraham** had **Sarah,** his wife, tell that she was his sister and not his wife in order to escape Pharaoh (Gen. 12:11-20). This Pharaoh acted in a manner characteristic of an Egyptian monarch of the time. In a magic formula found at the pyramid of Unas, a Pharaoh of the Fifth Dynasty, we find, "Then he (namely, the Pharaoh) takes away the wives from their husbands whither he will if desire seize his heart." Perhaps knowing this, **Abraham** lacked the faith in God who would have protected him and **Sarah** without having to resort to a half-truth.

Thus the conditions of the Land of Canaan and the surrounding kingdoms touched on **Abraham's** life and influenced some of his decisions. The giving of Hagar by **Sarah** to **Abraham** was also in accordance with the customs of the time. Nuzi was a city in Assyria in the same period of time and we can read of its marital customs.

Sarah's action in giving her Egyptian servant, Hagar, to her husband illustrates Nuzi customs. **Sarah** lost faith of becoming a mother herself (Gen. 16:1-16). Later, **Rachel** followed the same course (Gen. 30:1-4). Nuzi customs seemed to say that if a wife was barren, she would furnish her husband with a slave wife.

After **Sarah** had given birth to **Isaac**, she demanded that Hagar and her child be expelled. **Abraham** was reluctant to satisfy her demand. Nuzi law provided that a slave wife's son should not be put out of the father's family (from Walton, *Ancient Israelite Literature in its Cultural Context*).

Secular History at the Time of Abraham

Near the time of **Abraham** and at the time of the Egyptian ruler Sesostris I, a nobleman named Sinuhe became involved in political intrigue and had to leave Egypt and went to live in Canaan by escaping over the Princes wall (a wall built at the eastern border of Egypt to keep the Bedouins out). Much of what we know of the nomadic life

in Canaan is found in Sinuhe's diary. In his old age he is called back to Egypt and returned to the splendor there which included a bathroom and a real bed. Sinuhe's diary corresponds very well with what we find in the biblical account of the conditions **Abraham** found there.

In chapter 14 of Genesis, we find that four kings invaded Sodom and carried away Lot and his goods. (Read Chapter 14.) It is interesting that the kings listed and the cities of the plain were thought to be fictional by secular history. But archaeological clay tablets from the Kingdom of Ebla establish some of the words of Genesis 14: even the cities are cited in the same order.

Archaeological Evidence

Ebla Kingdom

(From McDowell, *Evidence that Demands a Verdict,* Vols. 1 and 2):

Since 1974, 17,000 tablets have been unearthed from the era of the Ebla Kingdom. The stone tablets refute previous *criticism* that the period described in the Mosaic narrative (1400 BC, a thousand years after the Ebla Kingdom) was a time prior to all knowledge of writing, and that customs and events of the Mosaic period were too advanced to have occurred at the time.

The Ebla archives refer to all five Cities of the Plain from Genesis 14 (Sodom, Gomorrah, Admah, Zeboiim, and Zoar), previously thought legendary. One tablet lists the cities in the exact same sequence as Genesis 14.

An archaeological find that relates to biblical criticism is the recently discovered Ebla tablets. The discovery was made in northern Syria by two professors from the University of Rome, Dr. Paolo Matthiae, an archaeologist, and Dr. Giovanni Petinato, an epigrapher. The excavation of the site, Tell Mardikh, began in 1964; in 1968 they uncovered a statue of King Ibbit-Lim. The inscription made a reference to Ishtar, the goddess who "shines brightly in Ebla." Ebla, at its height of power in 2300 BC, had a population of 260,000 people. It was destroyed in 2250 BC by Naram-Sin, grandson of Sargon the Great.

The proponents of the "Documentary Hypothesis" have taught in the past that the period described in the Mosaic narrative (1400 BC, a thousand years after the Ebla Kingdom) was a time prior to all knowledge of writing (see author's *More Evidence That Demands a Verdict*, 63). But Ebla shows that, a thousand years before Moses, laws, customs and events were recorded in writing in the same area of the world in which Moses and the patriarchs lived.

The higher critics have not only taught that it was a time prior to writing but also that the Priestly Code and legislation recorded in the Pentateuch were too far developed to have been written by Moses. It was alleged that the Israelites were too primitive at that time to have written them and that it wasn't until about the first half of the Persian period (538-331 BC) that such detailed legislation was recorded.

An additional example of the contribution of the Ebla discovery is in relation to Genesis 14, which for years has been considered to be historically unreliable. The victory of Abraham over Chedolaomer and the Mesopotamian kings has been described as fictitious and the five Cities of the Plain (Sodom, Gomorrah, Admah, Zeboiim and Zoar) as legendary.

Yet the Ebla archives refer to all five Cities of the Plain and on one tablet the Cities are listed in the exact same sequence as Genesis 14. The milieu of the tablets reflect the culture of the patriarchal period and depict that, before the catastrophe recorded in Genesis 14, the area was a flourishing region experiencing prosperity and success, as recorded in Genesis (*http://en.wikipedia.org/wiki/Ebla*).

Abraham, with God's help, along with the kings of the cities of the Valley of Siddim defeated Chedolaomer and the kings who were with him.

Later, **Abraham** was met by Melchizedek king of Salem (Jerusalem), who was a priest of God Most High and the type of Jesus. Melchizedek gave **Abraham** bread and wine and **Abraham** gave a tenth of all his spoils to Melchizedek. This meeting is also referred to by the author of Hebrews in chapters five and especially seven. Christ not being of the tribe of Levi could not be a priest unless there was a change of the priesthood, thus He is a priest after the order of Melchizedek. How could one understand what was being argued

in chapter seven unless he had a knowledge of the Old Testament Scriptures? As stated before, one needs knowledge of the Old Testament in order to understand completely the New Testament.

We all recall the episode of **Abraham** and Lot, found in Genesis 13, where Lot chose the fertile plain and lived among some of the most wicked people in the world, yet remained righteous himself. As for this lesson, we will concentrate on **Abraham** and his family. God made a covenant with **Abraham** in Genesis chapter 12 and reiterated in chapter 15. He promised that **Abraham's** descendants would inherit Canaan, and that in **Abraham's** "seed" all the nations of the earth would be blessed. Also in Chapter 15:13 God told **Abraham** that his descendants would be strangers in a land not their own and would be enslaved and oppressed **four hundred years**. This is a very important passage that gives us a clue as to when **Abraham** lived. For in Galatians 3:16-17 Paul says, "Now the promises were spoken to **Abraham** and to his seed. He does not say, 'And to seeds,' as referring to many, but to one, 'And to your seed,' that is Christ. What I am saying is this: the Law, which came **four hundred and thirty years later**, does not invalidate a covenant previously ratified by

God, so as to nullify the promise." Thus when the Old Law was given at Sinai (the Exodus), it was 430 years after the promise to **Abraham**. By adding these years to 1446 BC the time calculated to be the Exodus we get 1446 + 430 or around 1876 BC when **Abraham** was 75 years old or approximately 1951 BC when he was born (Beitzel). This date could be off by as much as 35 years in some calculations.

The next important event in **Abraham's** life was his faith shown in preparing to offer **Isaac**, upon the altar. Now **Abraham's** faith was mature and pleasing to God. One could ask, "How could God ask **Abraham** to sacrifice his own son?" One finds related in Hebrews 11:19, "He (**Abraham**) considered that God is able to raise *men* even from the dead; from which he also received

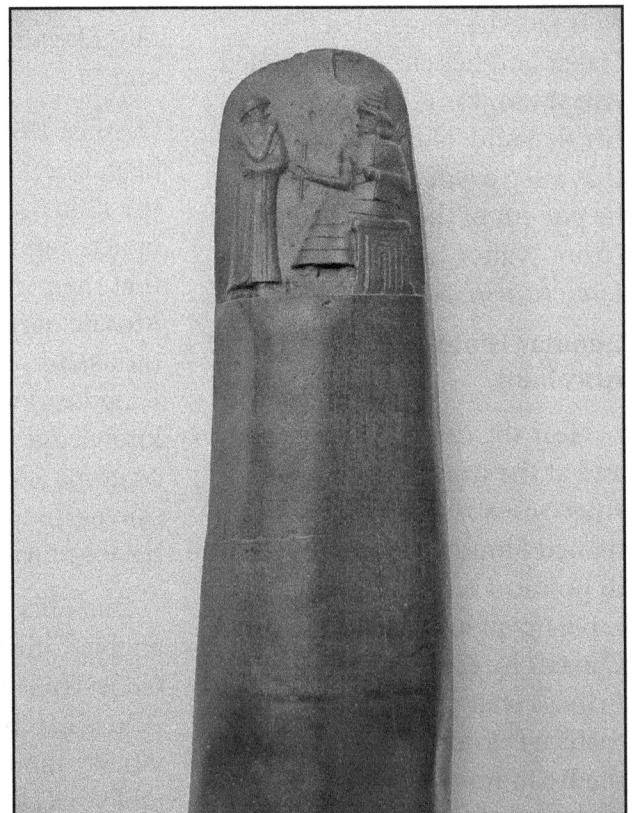

Law Code of Hammurabi

"Men of Whom the World Was Not Worthy"

him (**Isaac**) back as a type." As **Abraham** had never seen anyone raised from the dead, consider how much **faith** it took for him to offer **Isaac** whom God had promised, "In **Isaac** your descendants shall be called" (Gen. 21:12).

In Luke16:19-31 we have the account of Lazarus and the rich man that gives us another aspect of the *living* **Abraham**. When the righteous man Lazarus died, where did he go? He went to **Abraham's** bosom. Now if we had not studied about **Abraham** and his life and faith, how would we know who **Abraham** is and why he would be found in the "Paradise" portion of Hades? Not only that, he is recognizable, spoken of as father, and important in this realm. Let us take a closer look at what is said about **Abraham** in Hebrews 11:8-19. Truly **Abraham** is the **father of the faithful** and today rests in Paradise.

At this time, let us examine the man named "Hammurabi" who was the ruler of all Mesopotamia shortly after the death of **Abra-ham.** Hammurabi was important for his "code" of laws that we have preserved for us today in a Stela, that can be found in the Louvre in Paris. This law was very advanced and expressed "an eye for an eye" and severe punishments for physicians who committed malpractice. Hammurabi was one of the first great emperors of Mesopotamia, but his empire soon collapsed, having been mismanaged by his sons who were conquered by the Hittites.

Questions

1. Name a book in the New Testament that discusses lessons based on the Old Testament history of **Abraham**?

_____

2. What was **Abraham's** most outstanding trait? _____

3. Who was Melchizedek, and what is his significance to the Christian? _____

_____

4. Do we have any archaeological evidence of the existence of Sodom and the other cities of the Plain?

_____

5. What is the significance to Christians about the offering up of **Isaac?** _____

_____

6. What was God's covenant with **Abraham**? _____

_____

7. What was found in the magic formula of Unas? What was its significance?_____

_____

8. How is **Abraham** our spiritual father**?** _____

_____

9. **Abraham** had other sons by his concubine Keturah. What is the biblical significance of two of those, Midian and Sheba? _____

10. What nationality was formed from Ishmael's offspring and who was a world famous offspring? _____

_____

Assignment for Lesson 5

Read Genesis 11:26-23:1-20.

5

Isaac and Jacob

Genesis 24-37

Timeline: circa 1850-1700 BC

Points to Remember: By faith **Isaac** blessed **Jacob** and Esau regarding things to come. Hebrews 12:15-17—Let there be no immoral or godless person like Esau. **Jacob** wrestled with an angel of God and received a blessing with his name changed to Israel meaning "he who strives with God." By faith **Jacob**, as he was dying, blessed each of the sons of Joseph and worshipped.

Isaac and Jacob

Abraham in his old age realized the Lord had blessed him in every way. He did not want his son to take a daughter of the Canaanites, in whose land they lived, so he sent his servant to go to Haran to get a wife for **Isaac** from his relatives. So the servant placed his hand under the thigh of his master and swore to him concerning the matter. This was a custom of the times. This servant was guided by the Lord God to find the daughter of Bethuel, the son of Milcah and Nahor. There the beautiful story of **Rebekah,** the sister of Laban, unfolds. She is asked to go and follow **Abraham's** servant; realizing the thing is of God, she goes and becomes the wife of **Isaac** (Gen. 24). **Rebekah** was barren till **Isaac** prayed for her and God opened her womb. Then she began to carry twins who seemed to struggle together within.

She inquired of the Lord, and He told her that the older would serve the younger. Esau (the father of the Edomites) was born first, and **Jacob** came forth holding on to the heel of Esau. God saw even in the womb of **Rebekah** that Esau was not of the nature to be in the line of succession for the coming Messiah and chose **Jacob** to be the son of promise and in the line of the Christ. (Read Gen. 25:23.) Did God show partiality here?

One should also remember the episode of Esau being hungry and selling his birthright for a bowl of "red" stew. That is where he got the name "Edom." Thus Esau despised his birthright. In Hebrews 12:16-17 we read, "…that there be no immoral or ungodly person like Esau, who sold his own birthright for a single meal. For you know that even afterwards, when he desired to inherit the blessing, he was rejected, for he found no place for repentance."

There was a famine in the land (Gen 26:1-11). What did Isaac do that was similar to what his father Abraham had done? Did both of these situations involve the same Abimelech? (See insert on the next page.)

Isaac stayed in Gerar for a long time; his possessions, blessed by God, grew a hundredfold (Gen. 26). The Philistines began to envy him and began to stop up the wells that his father **Abraham** had dug. Then Abimelech sent him away to a nearby valley, and **Isaac** dug again the wells his father had dug. Again, the Philistine herdsmen began to contend with him over the water so he moved on. There, too, he was also hassled by the surrounding herdsmen and moved farther to Rehoboth, finally getting enough separation. Here he thanked the Lord for making room for his family and herds. This illustrates how **Abraham** and then **Isaac** were influenced by the peoples of Canaan where they were but wanderers. After moving to Beersheba, where the Lord blessed him, Abimelech came to see him and made a covenant of peace between them.

Seemingly, to prove God's foresight, Esau began to marry the daughters of the Hittites and brought grief upon **Isaac** and Rebekah.

In his old age **Isaac,** almost blind, was fooled by **Jacob** and Rebekah. He gave the best bless-

Abimelech

Meaning: my father a king, or father of a king.

This was the common name for Philistine kings, as "Pharaoh" was of the Egyptian kings.

This was the name of five biblical men:

1. The Philistine king of Gerar in the time of Abraham (Gen. 20:1-18). By an interposition of Providence, Sarah was delivered from his harem, and was restored to her husband Abraham. As a mark of respect, he gave to Abraham valuable gifts, and offered him a settlement in any part of his country; while at the same time he delicately and yet severely rebuked him for having practiced a deception upon him in pretending that Sarah was only his sister.

Among the gifts presented by the king were a thousand pieces of silver as a "covering of the eyes" for Sarah; i.e., either as an atoning gift and a testimony of her innocence in the sight of all, or rather for the purpose of procuring a veil for Sarah to conceal her beauty, and thus as a reproof to her for not having worn a veil which, as a married woman, she ought to have done.

A few years after this Abimelech visited Abraham, who had removed southward beyond his territory, and there entered into a league of peace and friendship with him. This league was the first of which we have any record. It was confirmed by a mutual oath at Beer-sheba (Gen. 21:22-34).

2. A king of Gerar in the time of Isaac, probably the son of the preceding (Gen. 26:1-22). Isaac sought refuge in his territory during a famine, and there he acted a part with reference to his wife Rebekah similar to that of his father Abraham with reference to Sarah. Abimelech rebuked him for the deception, which he accidentally discovered. Isaac settled for a while here, and prospered. Abimelech desired him, however, to leave his territory, which Isaac did. Abimelech afterwards visited him when he was encamped at Beer-sheba, and expressed a desire to renew the covenant which had been entered into between their fathers (Gen. 26:26-31).

3. A son of Gideon (Judg. 9:1), **who was proclaimed king after the death of his father** (Judg. 8:33-9:6). One of his first acts was to murder his brothers, seventy in number, "on one stone," at Ophrah. Only one, named Jotham, escaped. Abimelech was an unprincipled, ambitious ruler, often engaged in war with his own subjects. When engaged in reducing the town of Thebez, which had revolted, he was struck mortally on his head by a millstone, thrown by the hand of a woman from the wall above. Perceiving that the wound was mortal, he desired his armor-bearer to thrust him through with his sword, that it might not be said he had perished by the hand of a woman (Judg. 9:50-57).

4. The son of Abiathar, and high priest in the time of David (1 Chron. 18:16). In the parallel passage (2 Sam. 8:17), we have the name Ahimelech, and Abiathar, the son of Ahimelech. This most authorities consider the more correct reading.

5. Achish, king of Gath, in the title of Psalm 34. (Compare 1 Sam. 21:10-15.) (*www.christiananswers.net/bible*).

ing to **Jacob** instead of to Esau, his favorite. **Jacob** put on goat skin over his arms so he would appear as Esau who was hairy. Esau bore a grudge for this and said he was going to kill **Jacob**. Why should God then bless **Jacob** who had deceived his father? Because it was from God all along that **Jacob** should be the son in the line of Christ. **Jacob** was then sent to Haran to live with Laban, Rebekah's brother, until Esau's fury should subside.

By Faith Jacob Blessed the Sons of Joseph (Gen. 28-35)

Although **Jacob** obtained his blessing by trickery, we know that Esau sold his birthright to him. In Hebrews 12:16-17, we read that Esau was a godless, impenitent, and immoral person. Also, it was God who chose **Jacob** to continue the lineage of Christ.

Jacob obeyed his father **Isaac** and also went back to Paddan-aram (Syria) to find a wife from **Abraham's** relatives, while Esau married wives of Ishmael. On his way **Jacob** had a dream of a ladder reaching into heaven with angels ascending and descending with the Lord (God the Father) standing above. God reiterated the promise given to **Abraham** concerning the land and nation that would now come to **Jacob's** descendants. And **Jacob** called the name of the place which had previously been called Luz, "Bethel" (the house of God), and **Jacob** made a vow that the Lord would be his God. **Jacob** would keep this promise and his faith grew.

God then blessed **Jacob** while he worked for Laban. **Jacob** eventually married both Rachel and Leah because of Laban's trickery. And because of the initial barrenness of Rachel, he had children of Leah and the handmaids of Rachel and Leah. This act was a custom in Canaan. Then God opened Rachel's womb; and she bore two sons, Joseph and Benjamin. Thus **Jacob** became the father of twelve sons who themselves began the twelve tribes of Israel.

God told **Jacob** to return home, and **Jacob** fled with his family and possessions from Laban. However, Rachel stole her fathers' family teraphim (household idols) and Laban came looking for them because they symbolized his power as head of the family. What did Rachel do to hide them (Gen. 31)?

This episode conforms very well with the tablets from cities like Nuzi and Ebla which relate the customs of the times.

Jacob wrestled with a man (Jesus, angel?) to a draw. The man dislocated **Jacob's** hip joint, but **Jacob** held on till he was blessed. The man blessed him and changed his name to **Israel** meaning "he who strives with God." **Jacob** promised to worship only Jehovah. Future references in this book will continue to use the name **Jacob** rather than Israel to distinguish between the man and the nation.

Jacob reunites with Esau and settles in the land of Canaan, at first near Shechem, and then in Bethel. When **Jacob** arrives in Canaan, he puts away all the foreign gods from his household just as he promised God. Then God blesses **Jacob** and reasserts the promises given to **Abraham.** Though **Jacob's** early adult life was marred by the deception of his father, his faith grew; and by the end of his life he was able through his faith to bless the children of Joseph and tell of things to come.

Jacob became the father of the twelve tribes of Israel. His eleventh and twelfth sons were from Rachael, and **Jacob** loved Joseph and Benjamin more than all the others. When Joseph was young, **Jacob** had a coat of many colors made for Joseph. (See the Ben Hasan painting in the next lesson which might depict what this coat looked like.) That coat and Joseph's dream of seeing his brothers bow down to him, made his brothers jealous. They then had Joseph sold into slavery where he eventually became second to Pharaoh in Egypt. Joseph will be studied more closely in the next lesson.

Judah, one of the sons of **Jacob,** would be chosen by God to be in the lineage of Christ. **Judah,** being deceived by **Tamar,** lay with her. God chose to have **Tamar** be brought in as the mother of **Perez** in the lineage of Christ. **Tamar's** story is a remarkable one (Gen. 38). Following is a chart of **Tamar** and the other notable women that Matthew included in the lineage of Christ (from http:www.lifeofchrist.com/life/genealogy/luke.html

Women in Christ's Genealogy

Matthew included five women in his genealogy of Christ. This is notable since it was not customary for Jews to include women in their records. Even more remarkable is the fact that Matthew included some women who had disreputable histories. The five women included were: Tamar, Rahab, Ruth, Bathsheba, and Mary.

Tamar: Genesis 38:6-30

Tamar was the daughter-in-law of Judah. She was a childless widow, who was given to her brother-in-law after her husband's death. By this marriage, her offspring would continue the name and inheritance of the deceased. Such a union was later called a Leverite marriage (Deut 25:5-6). Unfortunately, Tamar's brother-in-law refused to have proper relations with her. God killed him for this. Afterwards, Judah would not give Tamar to any of his other sons. So Tamar disguised herself as a harlot and seduced Judah. Through him, she became the mother of Perez.

Rahab: Joshua 2:1-24

Rahab was a harlot who lived in Jericho. She hid the spies of Joshua. Because of this, the Israelites spared her life when they conquered Jericho. She later became the wife of Salmon, and the mother of Boaz. Rahab's faith was later commended (Heb 11:30-31).

Ruth: Ruth 1:1-4:22

Ruth was a foreigner from the land of Moab. She was the widow of a Jew. Her mother-in-law, Naomi, also lived in Moab. Naomi journeyed to Israel after her family died. Ruth's devotion was extraordinary. She left her own country to follow Naomi. While in Israel, Ruth was married to Boaz, one of Naomi's relatives. Ruth later became the mother of Obed, the grandfather of David the King.

Bathsheba: 2 Samuel 11:1-27

Bathsheba was the wife of Uriah the Hittite, who was a soldier in the army of King David. She and David had an adulterous affair. When David discovered Bathsheba was pregnant, he tried to cover it up by summoning Uriah home from war, hoping that Uriah would have relations with his wife. Uriah came home to Jerusalem, but refused to lay with Bathsheba as long as the armies of Israel were at war. So, David sent Uriah back into battle, with orders that Uriah should be withdrawn from when the fighting became fierce. After Uriah was slain in this manner, David took Bathsheba as his own wife. God punished them for this by killing their first child. Bathsheba later became the mother of Solomon.

Mary: Matthew 1:18-25; Luke 1:26-56

Mary was the mother of Jesus and the wife of Joseph. She was a virgin when Jesus was conceived by the Holy Spirit. Joseph was betrothed to Mary when he discovered she was pregnant. He intended to put her away secretly because this was shameful. However, an angel told Joseph what had happened. So Joseph took Mary as his wife, and kept her as a virgin until she gave birth to Jesus. During her pregnancy, Mary spent time with her relative Elizabeth, who was the mother of John the Baptist (Luke 1:39-56). Mary was not a perpetual virgin, as she later became the mother of other sons and daughters (Matt. 13:55-56).

Questions

1. How did **Isaac** repeat his father's deception with the king of the Philistines, Abimelech? _____

   _____

2. Why did **Isaac** prefer the usual meat of Esau to what **Jacob** served?_____

   _____

3. What acts of faith were shown by **Isaac** during his life? _____

   _____

4. Why do you think Moses by inspiration told the story of **Jacob** stealing the blessing from **Isaac**? Did God approve? (See Gen. 25:21-26.) _____

   _____

5. Was **Jacob** right in loving Joseph more than his other sons, and did this favoritism contribute to what happened to Joseph? _____

6. How did **Jacob's** faith grow? _____

7. What attributes of Esau were not pleasing to God? _____

   _____

8. **Judah** was chosen to be in the lineage of Christ, and it passed to his Son, **Perez**. Who was **Perez's** mother, and what was the circumstance of his birth? _____

   _____

9. Which one of **Jacob's** sons became preeminent? _____

Asignment for Lesson 6

Read Genesis 39-50

Joseph

Hebrews 11:22; Genesis 37-50

6

Timeline: ca 1800-1600 BC

Points to Remember: By faith Joseph, when he was dying, made mention of the Exodus that was to come many years later. Most of the life of Joseph is spent in Egypt. The Egyptians descended from Ham through Mizraim.

Joseph

As children we studied the early life of Joseph who was born to **Jacob** and Rachel (Jacob's favorite wife). **Jacob** showed favoritism to Joseph, and Joseph's dream that predicted his ascendancy over the older sons of the other wives caused jealousy. The brothers then plotted to get rid of him. They stripped Joseph of his coat of many colors and threw him into a pit. Although some wanted to kill him, **Judah** suggested that they sell him to some passing tradesmen. Thus Joseph, through no sin on his part, was taken to Egypt and sold into slavery.

In Genesis 39:1 we read, "Now Joseph had been taken down to Egypt; and Potiphar, an Egyptian officer of Pharaoh, the captain of the bodyguard, bought him from the Ishmaelites, who had taken him down there." We all know the story of how Joseph was so successful in running Potiphar's house that he was put in charge of all of Potiphar's affairs. Joseph, however, was accused by Potiphar's wife of impropriety with her. Joseph ran away, even leaving his tunic, but landed in prison. He later rose to be a trusted servant in prison and interpreted the cupbearer's dream.

With God's help, Joseph interpreted Pharaoh's dream. Pharaoh gave Joseph the daughter of the priest of On for his wife. He also gave him gifts that were significant and which we will discuss when we begin to determine which Pharaoh was in Egypt at the time of Joseph. Joseph was able in this position to prepare Egypt for the coming famine.

Although Joseph's brothers meant their actions for harm, God meant it for good so Joseph could save his family from famine. When Joseph's brothers came to Egypt for help in the famine, they did not recognize Joseph. Joseph at first played mind games with them, but finally he let them know who he was. With the blessing of the Pharaoh, the Israelites were given some of the best land to live in (Goshen).

With his Egyptian wife, Asenath, Joseph had two sons whom he named Manasseh and Ephraim. When Jacob grew old he blessed Joseph's sons, and they became the head of half tribes. Jacob gave preeminence to Joseph's sons.

Ben Hasan Painting of Semitic people coming to Egypt.

After many years a new pharaoh arose who did not know Joseph and the Israelites became slaves of the Egyptians

Egypt and the Pharaohs at the Time of Joseph

Who were the Egyptians? As stated before, the Egyptians descended from Noah through Ham and Mizraim (*New Illustrated Bible Dictionary*). What pharaohs were ruling during the time of Joseph and the captivity? No doubt some Christians will be wary of trying to discover something the Bible has not clearly revealed, but these questions have been asked and studied for centuries. This writer believes one can come away with his or her faith strengthened if the Bible can be confirmed with data that has been supplied to us by secular history, such as in the Tel el-Amarna letters, found in 1888. In those letters Ebed-Hepa, a vassal king of Egypt living in Jerusalem, appeals for help against invaders called the Habiru. Some historians think Habiru seems to stand for the Hebrews (or some of the other descendants of Eber) and shows some snippets of interaction between them and the Egyptians. At any rate, the Egyptians and the Hebrews did have 215 years (Septuagint) of living together in one relationship or another.

In order to know who the ruler of Egypt was at the time of Joseph, one must learn something about the history of Egypt and then count backwards from the Exodus in order to determine the pharaoh. Who was the first

and was the founder of the first dynasty of Egypt around 3000 BC. Many historians think these names belonged to the same person who lived around 3000 BC.

(For more on this topic I will refer you to *http://www.mnsu.edu/emeuseum/prehistory/egypt/history/people/mense.html*).

It appears that the Israelites were actually in Egypt for 215 years. Since the date of the Exodus can be determined easier than the timeline for Joseph, we will start there and count backwards. When was the Exodus? In 1 Kings 6:1 we read, "and it came to pass in the four hundred and eightieth year after the children of Israel were come out of the land of Egypt, in the fourth year of Solomon's reign over Israel, in the month of Zif, which is the second month that he began to build the house of the Lord." So if we can know when the temple was started, then we

tians kept good records except during the years of the Hyksos rulers. In 1445 BC, the Egyptian ruler was probably Amenhotep II: we will read more of him later as we study Moses, but we now want to establish which ruler was in power at the time of Joseph.

The historian Beitzel gives the best timeline that conforms to Egyptian and biblical history, as excerpted from *Archaeology & the Old Testament* by Alfred Hoerth:

In Exodus 12:40 it appears that the Israelites came to dwell in Egypt 430 years before the Exodus (1446 BC) or around 1876 BC. However, the Septuagint version and also Paul in Galatians 3:17 interprets this as 215 years with the other 215 years composed of the time of Abraham's and his descendants' wanderings prior to the time Jacob and his family went down into Egypt. So it appears that Joseph was in Egypt about 215 years before 1446 BC or around 1660 BC.

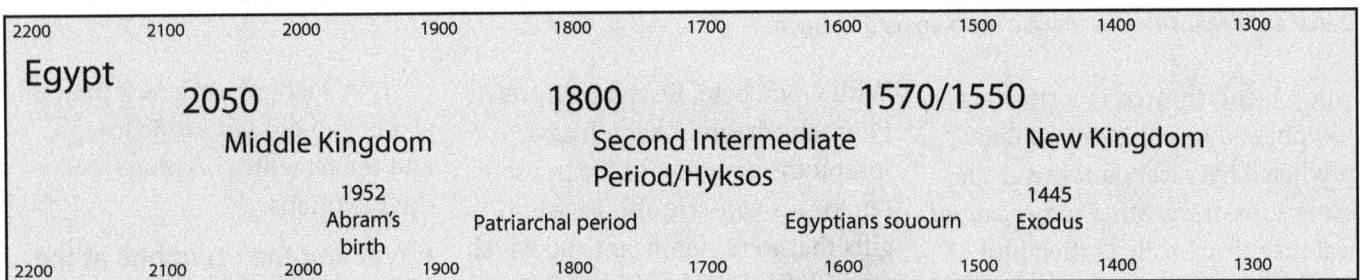

2200	2100	2000	1900	1800	1700	1600	1500	1400	1300

Egypt

2050 — Middle Kingdom

1800 — Second Intermediate Period/Hyksos

1570/1550 — New Kingdom

1952 Abram's birth

Patriarchal period

Egyptians souourn

1445 Exodus

2200	2100	2000	1900	1800	1700	1600	1500	1400	1300

pharaoh (king) of Egypt? History and fable are mixed during this period, making the search for the name of the first king confusing. Probably the first king was Menes, also possibly known as Aha, the Scorpion King, or Narmer. These may have been all different names for one person. The Greek historian Herodotus wrote that Menes was the ruler who unified Egypt

can know when the Exodus was. Scholar's have identified the fourth year of Solomon's rule as 966 BC (Gleason, *A Survey of Old Testament Introduction*, 1974, p. 223) Using this year of 966 and adding 480 years, one gets 1446 BC as the year of the Exodus.

We have the dates of the Egyptian Pharaohs because the Egyp-

corresponding to the reign of the Hyksos, rulers of foreign lands (Beitzel).

Egypt During the 15th Dynasty

As a result of the weakened positions of the 13th and 14th Dynasties, Egypt lay open to any outside aggression. At around 1800 BC, Egypt was invaded by a group of Canaanites, whose leader was called HqA-xAs.wt, ruler of the foreign land, or Hyksos (www.swarzentrover.com/cotor/bible/timelines/egypt; and Hoerth, 57).

The Hyksos easily conquered Avaris as well as Memphis, causing the end of both the 13th and 14th Dynasties and founding their own dynasty, the 15th Dynasty. It appears that Joseph came into Egypt during this period. Sir Alan Gardner summed up the Hyksos position this way: ". . . the rare remains of the Hyksos kings point . . . to an earnest endeavor to conciliate the inhabitants and to ape the attributes and the trappings of the Pharaohs they dislodged." The names and even the order of their kings is confusing, and their capital city (Avaris) has only recently been identified in the eastern delta. The Egyptians made a concerted effort to purge their (Hyksos) stay from Egyptian history (Hoerth, *Archaeology and the Old Testament*, 1998) Thus, the pharaoh of Joseph's ascendency may never be known.

Joseph stayed in Egypt and lived one hundred and ten years (Gen. 50:22-26). As he was about to die, Joseph prophesied that God would take care of his family and bring them out of Egypt into the Promised Land. Joseph also made the sons of Israel swear to carry his bones out of Egypt. This request, found in Hebrews 11:22, was given by faith. "By faith Joseph, when he was dying, made mention of the exodus of the sons of Israel, and gave orders concerning his bones." Thus we have the remarkable account of Joseph's life, one of the faithful heroes of the Old Testament.

Questions

1. To whom was Joseph sold into slavery? _____

2. What happened with Joseph's master's wife? _____
_____

3. Describe what Joseph did while in prison and how long he was there. _____
_____

4. What dealings did Pharaoh's cupbearer and baker have with Joseph? _____
_____

5. What was Pharaoh's dream, and how did Joseph interpret it? _____
_____

6. What reward was given to Joseph for the successful interpretation of the dreams? _____
_____

7. Who did Joseph marry to bear his two children? _____

8. The famine of the dream affected more than Egypt. Who went to Egypt to buy grain, and what happened? _____

9. What surety did Reuben give to **Jacob** that Reuben would bring Benjamin back? _____
_____

10. Describe the blessings given to Ephraim and Manasseh. _____
_____

11. Tell how Joseph displayed his faith when he was close to dying. _____
_____

Assignment for Lesson 7

Read Exodus 1-40.

Timeline: 1525-1405 BC

Points to Remember: Moses esteemed the reproach of Christ, greater than treasures of Egypt; meekness is not weakness; Moses, the lawgiver and greatest prophet; the miraculous overthrow of the

Dream stele of Thutmose IV

Egyptians by Jehovah was known by the countries of the region; even though one may feel inadequate as Moses did, God may need him for His purpose. Moses's life can be divided into three periods: the forty years in Egypt, the forty years in Midian, and the forty years in the wilderness.

Moses

"Now there arose up a new king over Egypt, which knew not Joseph" (Exod. 1:8). The Egyptian king then said to his people that the Israelites were multiplying and needed to be controlled to prevent them from throwing in with the enemies of Egypt in time of war. They afflicted the Israelites with heavy tasks, but the more they afflicted them, the more they grew. Finally, the king spoke to the Hebrew midwives, Shiphrah and Puah, to kill all the male children whom they helped to deliver. But the midwives feared God and did not do as instructed and reported that the Hebrew women delivered their own male children before the midwives arrived. Therefore, God dealt well with the midwives (Exod. 1:15-21). Pharaoh then charged his people to cast all the male children into the river. A young child (Moses) was placed by his mother and sister in an ark of bulrushes; and after being found by the daughter of Pharaoh, he was raised in Pharaoh's house as her son. Moses's mother was hired to be the nursemaid for her own son.

One day as Moses grew and learned from his mother that he was a Hebrew, he saw an Egyptian beating one of his Hebrew brethren. Moses killed the Egyptian and hid him in the sand.

When Pharaoh heard of this, he sought to kill Moses, but Moses fled and went to dwell in the land of Midian (Arabia). Moses met Jethro there, who gave Zipporah to Moses for a wife.

The pharaoh of Egypt died and God, after hearing the groaning of His people, appeared to Moses in a burning bush. He asked Moses to go back and lead His people. Moses was meek. It took persuasion from God, the giving of signs, and Aaron his brother, to convince Moses that he was up to the task. As Moses and his family were traveling, the Lord sought to kill Moses because Moses neglected to circumcise Gershom, his son. Fortunately, Zipporah circumcised Gershom and saved Moses from the wrath of God.

A Bible student should know the rest of the story. Moses and Aaron obeyed God and told Pharaoh that God had said, "Let My people go." The Lord God brought ten plagues upon the Egyptians by the power of God, the last being the worst—the death of the first-born son of all the Egyptians:

1. Water into blood
2. Frogs
3. Lice
4. Swarms of insects
5. Pestilence on livestock

6. Boils
7. Hail and fire
8. Locusts
9. Darkness
10. Death of the firstborn of Egypt

God instituted the Passover to protect the Israelites, and finally the Pharaoh agreed to let the Israelites depart. Moses, with God's help, led the Israelites through the miraculously divided Red Sea into the Wilderness of Paran; the entire Egyptian army, with all its chariots, horses, and men, was destroyed. Moses then was given the Ten Commandments by God on Mount Sinai. It is important to note the Ten Commandments and to show that one of them is not reiterated in the New Testament. That one, the sabbath law, is not to be followed by Christians. The following table lists the Ten Commandments and gives the New Testament references where nine are again commanded:

1. You shall have no other gods before me (**Acts 19:26; Matt. 4:10**).

2. You shall not make an idol to worship (**1 Cor. 5:11;10:7, 14**).

3. You shall not take the name of the lord God in vain (**Matt. 6:9; 12:36; James 2:7**).

4. Remember the sabbath day to keep it holy. **No Scripture in the New Testament.**

5. Honor your father and mother, that your days may be long (**Matt. 15:3-4**).

6. You shall not murder (**Matt. 5:21; Rom. 13:9**).

7. You shall not commit adultery (**Matt. 5:27; Rom. 13:9**).

8. You shall not steal (**Rom. 13:9**).

9. You shall not bear false witness (**Matt. 19:18; Acts 6:13**).

10. You shall not covet (**Rom. 13:9**).

In Numbers 13, we read about the sending of the twelve spies to spy out Canaan for the conquest. Only two spies (Joshua and Caleb) came back with a good report, while the other ten said that there were giants in the land and that the Israelites would fail. For doubting God's power to defeat the Canaanites, the Israelites had to wander forty years in the wilderness.

Later, Moses prepared to lead His people into the Promised Land. He was prevented by God, however, because he struck the rock instead of speaking to the rock as commanded by God (Deut. 32:48-52). Moses died on Mount Pisgah after seeing the Promised Land. Yet, Moses is remembered as God's greatest prophet and a man of great faith. In Deuteronomy 34:10 it is written, "And there arose not a prophet since in Israel like unto Moses, whom the Lord knew face to face, in all the signs and the wonders, which the Lord sent him to do in the land of Egypt to Pharaoh, and to all his servants, and to all his land, and in all that mighty hand, and in all the great terror which Moses shewed in the sight of all Israel."

Also, in Numbers 12:3, we read, "Now the man Moses was very meek above all the men which were upon the face of the earth."

Although Jehovah gave the Law **to** Moses, it was forever and consistently called the Law **of** Moses. He wrote the first five books of the Old Testament by inspiration. In Psalms 77:20, David recalled that God worked through Moses, "You (God) led Your people like a flock by the hand of Moses and Aaron." Moses was at times maddened by the murmurings of the people as in Numbers 20:1-13. It was at Meribah that Moses, angry at the Israelites because of their murmuring for water, struck the rock to bring forth water instead of speaking to the rock as God had commanded.

Much more could be said about the great man of faith and prophet, Moses, but one needs to look at the country of Egypt from which the people of God were led to the Exodus.

The Pharaohs of Egypt at the Time of the Exodus

When was the Exodus, and who was the pharaoh who was ruling? This is a most perplexing question and one that may never be answered to everyone's satisfaction. The following conclusions are based on the assumption that the Exodus was either in the year 1445 or 1446 BC. The exact dates of most of the pharaohs are not known accurately. Certain known facts will be given to substantiate these conclusions, but some scholars disagree.

In 1 Kings 6:11, we are told, "And it came to pass in the four hundred and eightieth year after the sons of Israel came out of the land of Egypt, in the fourth year of Solomon's reign over Israel—that he began to build the house of the Lord." Thus 480 years before the fourth year of the reign of Solomon was the Exodus. Scholars tell us that in 966 BC, Solomon began his temple (Gleason, *A Survey of Old Testament Introduction*, 1974, p. 223). So if one adds 480 to 966, one gets 1446 BC as the year of the Exodus. At this point it must be reiterated that even though it appears clear to this author what the date of the Exodus was, some scholars disagree as to that date and who the pharaoh was at that time. A lot of evidence suggests that this was Pharaoh Amenhotep II.

From whom did Amenhotep II descend? When comparing Exodus 7:7 with Acts 7:23, we learn that Moses was in Midian for forty years. If the pharaoh of Exodus 1:8, 22, and 2:23 are all the same person, he would have had to reign for over forty years. Thutmose III, who was co-regent with his step-mother Hatshepsut for several years and then ruled on his own, is the only pharaoh to have ruled long enough (54 years) to have been on the throne at the time of Moses's flight and to die shortly before his return to Egypt.

St. Peter's Square at the Vatican displays the obelisk from Thutmose IV of Egypt, eighth pharaoh of the 18th dynasty

Hatshepsut has been sought out by the Feminist movement and given the title "the first great woman in history." She is depicted in a 2005 computer game, "Civilization IV." She built the first tomb in the Valley of the Kings called Djeser-Djeseru, and it was a magnificent symmetrical architectural structure. She died as she was approaching middle age around 1482 BC, and Thutmose III assumed the throne by himself.

Thutmose III is regarded as one the greatest of Egypt's pharaohs. He ruled around 1504-1450 BC. He is also called the Napoleon of Egypt for all his military exploits, having captured 350 cities during his rule; and he changed Egypt into a superpower in the Ancient World. Thutmose III was probably the pharaoh who ordered the killing of all the Israelite males, and he had a daughter who found the child Moses and raised him. Thutmose III married the daughter of his stepmother, Hatshepsut.

Thus, one can reasonably conclude that Thutmose III was the pharaoh from whom Moses fled, and that Amenhotep II was the pharaoh of the Exodus. Amenhotep II, the son of Thutmose III, succeeded him and would have been in power in 1446 BC. Furthermore, it has been learned that the son of Amenhotep II, Thutmose IV, was not the legitimate heir. An article by Jimmy Dunn gives the story of the dream stele of Thutmose IV, who dreamed he became pharaoh although not the first in line (*www.toutegypt.net/feature-stories/tuthmosis4.htm*).

The firstborn son of Amenhotep II had evidently died prior to taking the throne. This fact would agree with Exodus 12:29 which states that Pharaoh's firstborn son was killed during the Passover (Allen Turner, *http://allanturner.com/pharoah.html*).

Archaeological evidence of Thutmose IV's reign can be seen

"Men of Whom the World Was Not Worthy"

in an obelisk that was quarried to be placed at Karnak. It now resides in St. Peter's Square in the Vatican.

Thus, Amenhotep II was probably the pharaoh of the Exodus, according to Allan Turner in *Who Was the Pharaoh of the Exodus (http://allanturner.com/pharoah.html)*. After the destruction of Amenhotep's army in the Red Sea, history tells us that the pharaoh was unable to carry out any invasions or extensive military operations for several years.

This circumstance is exactly what one would expect from a pharaoh who had lost almost all of his cavalry, chariotry, and army at the Red Sea. The Bible does not tell us if the pharaoh, himself, was killed in the Red Sea.

Questions

1. What can we learn from the study of Moses's life? _____

_____

2. How could Moses be mighty and meek at the same time? _____

_____

3. What was Moses's greatest strength and his greatest weakness? _____

_____

4. The midwives disobeyed the Pharaoh and told him a lie. Is lying ever approved by God? _____

_____

5. Who could have been the pharaoh of the Exodus? _____

6. Why is Moses the greatest prophet? _____

_____

7. How can we describe the meekness of Moses? _____

_____

8. Why was Moses not allowed to enter the Promised Land? What lesson can we learn from that? _____

_____

9. In Hebrews 11, we find several examples of Moses's faith. What are they? _____

_____

Assignment for Lesson 8

Read Joshua 1-24.

Timeline: 1446-1380 BC

Points to Remember: The Lord told Joshua to be strong and courageous. With God's help, Joshua conquered Canaan. At the end of his life, Joshua stated, "As for me and my house, we will serve the Lord." God stopped the sun and moon to help Joshua defeat the five kings.

Joshua

Joshua and **Rahab** will be studied together in one lesson because they were contemporaries and there is not much recorded in the Bible about **Rahab**. Joshua was born in Egypt. He went through the great events of the Passover, and the crossing of the Red Sea. He became Moses's assistant and went with Moses at times into the mountain when Moses was to talk to God (Exod. 24:13).

Perhaps Joshua's two most memorable deeds were: (1) being one of the spies sent into Canaan, and (2) his leading of God's people in the battle and defeat of Jericho. In Numbers 13, God commanded Moses to seek out leaders of all the tribes and Hoshea was chosen from the tribe of Ephraim. In verse 16 we find that Moses called Hoshea, Joshua. Only Joshua and Caleb gave a good report, saying that Israel could take the land. Be-

cause of the lack of faith of the other eight spies, God made all of the Israelites wander in the wilderness for forty years. Joshua, Caleb, Moses, and Aaron were among the few faithful over twenty of age who were allowed to survive the wilderness wandering.

After Moses was not allowed to enter the Promised Land and later died, Joshua was appointed to lead God's people into Canaan. God spoke to Joshua and told him to conquer the land and be "strong and courageous." In Joshua 3:7-17 God said, "This day I will begin to exalt you in the sight of all Israel that they may know that just as I have been with Moses, I will be with you." So God gave to Joshua the power to stop the Jordan River which allowed the Israelites to cross on dry land. Joshua, with the help of God, defeated kings who were literally giants; and he eventually conquered all the land that God had promised to Israel. One should look at a map of Canaan and become familiar with the nations and their locations. But the battles were not without problems and most were of the Israelites' own making. In Joshua 9:1-14, the Gibeonites tricked Joshua and the Israelites because the Israelites "did not ask for the council of the Lord." But overall, Joshua was a great leader who followed God.

Rahab

When Joshua crossed the Jordan, he began planning to take Jericho. The hearts of the Amorites and Canaanites melted when they heard how the Lord had dried up the waters of the Jordan River. He sent spies into Jericho where they met **Rahab,** a harlot of the Canaanites who had heard of God's power over the Egyptians and believed He was the true God.

Rahab hid the spies from the king of Jericho and was promised to be spared when Jericho was destroyed.

Jericho was an ancient city on a hill heavily fortified with, not one, but two high walls. It was almost impregnable with the military means available then. After the Israelites obeyed God and marched around Jericho for seven days, the walls of Jericho fell down and out, making it possible for Joshua's army to march straight up and into the city. Now one can see the ruins of the old city close by the modern Jericho.

We are told in Hebrews 11:31 that **Rahab** and her family did not perish with the rest of the inhabitants because of her "faith and works." Joshua proclaimed a curse on whoever would rebuild Jericho. That man would lose his firstborn when he laid the foundation and his youngest when he put up the gates (Josh. 6:26). Interestingly many years later, "In his days Hiel the Bethelite built Jericho; he laid its foundation with the *loss* of Abiram his firstborn, and set up its gates with the *loss* of his youngest son, Segub, according to the word of the Lord, which He spoke by Joshua the son of Nun" (1 Kings 16:34).

Thus, Joshua led the Israelites to conquer the land. In Joshua 21:44-45 one reads, "There stood not a man of all their (the Israelites) enemies before them; the Lord delivered all their enemies into their hand....There failed not ought of any good thing which the Lord had spoken unto the house of Israel; all came to pass" (Josh. 21:44-45). Thus God's land promises to Abraham were fulfilled at that time. One should not be looking for a future fulfillment of the land promise. Joshua divided the land among the twelve tribes of Israel. On a map, look at all the lands given to Manasseh and Ephraim, the sons of Joseph. Where is the land for Levi? How can this be explained? See Joshua 13:33.

In his farewell speech in Joshua 24:14-15, Joshua charged his people to follow God and declares the immortal words, "And if it seems evil unto you to serve the Lord, choose you this day whom you will serve; whether the gods which your fathers served . . . that were beyond the river or the gods of the Amorites, in whose land you dwell: but as for me and my house, **we will serve the Lord**." In verse 31 of the same chapter we read, "And Israel served the Lord all the days of Joshua and all the days of the elders who survived Joshua, and had known all the deeds of the Lord which

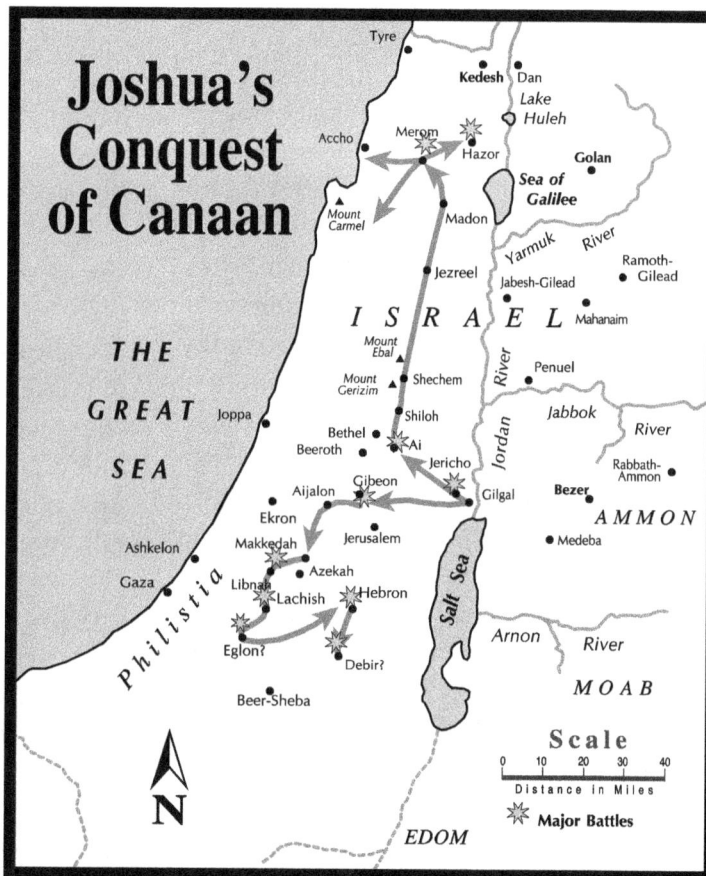

Joshua's Conquest of Canaan

He had done for Israel." However, soon afterwards we find in Judges 2:11-12 that Israel did evil in the sight of the Lord and served the Baals, and forsook the Lord the God of their fathers, who had brought them out of the land of Egypt, followed other gods, and provoked the Lord to anger.

What an excellent example of faith Joshua showed in his words and in his life.

The World at the Time of Joshua

The rest of the world at the time of Joshua still was in the control of the Egyptians and the various rulers of Mesopotamia. But, at this time, the Canaanites, Moabites, Midianites, and Ammonites were the peoples that influenced the Israelites the most. In Judges 1:21 we read, "But the sons of Benjamin did not drive out the Jebusites who lived in Jerusalem; so the Jebusites have lived with the sons of Benjamin in Jerusalem to this day." Most of the other Canaanite tribes were also not completely driven out of the Promised Land as God had commanded.

Amorites and Canaanites

In Genesis 10:15-17, we read, "And Canaan became the father of Sidon, his firstborn, and Heth and the Jebusite and the Amorite and the Girgashite and the Hivite. . . ." In Genesis 15:13-21, God told **Abram** that his descendants, in the fourth generation, would return to Canaan and take possession of it then because the iniquity of the Amorite was not yet complete. It appears that the term "Amorite" was sometimes used to describe the whole of the Canaanites. In

Genesis 34:2 and Genesis 48:22 the Hivites are also said to be Amorites.

The Jebusites occupied Jebus (Jerusalem) at the time of Joshua's conquest. In Joshua 10 we are told their king was Adonizedek. He participated with five other Amorite kings to attack Gibeon whose inhabitants were then allied with Israel. Joshua was called by Gibeon to assist them. He was told by God that the Amorites were given into his hand, and he defeated them with a great slaughter. It was in this battle that Joshua asked God to stop the sun and moon until the nation of Israel avenged themselves of their enemies. Continuing on in Joshua 10, we read, "And the sun stopped in the middle of the sky, and did not hasten to go down for about a whole day. And there was no day like that before it or after it, when the Lord listened to the voice of a man; for the Lord fought for Israel." One can see why Joshua was included in the list of worthies in Hebrews 11:30 by his faith and deeds, if not by name.

Although Adonizedek and his army were defeated, it was not until **David** came to power that Jebus (Jerusalem) fell. It was the strongest fortress left in Israel. When **David** and his men went up against Jebus, the men of the city said, "You shall not come in here, but the blind and the lame shall turn you away." Nevertheless **David** with God's help entered Jebus through the water tunnel and captured it. He renamed the city Jerusalem and it was then called the city of **David**.

Canaanites

The Canaanites were descended from Canaan, the son of Ham. In Genesis 9:22-29 we read, "And Ham, the father of Canaan, saw the nakedness of his father (Noah), and told his two brothers outside." His two brothers acted righteously and covered Noah, who had become drunk from the wine of his vineyard. "When Noah awoke from his wine, he knew what his youngest had done to him. So he said, 'Cursed be Canaan; a servant of servants he shall be to his brothers.'" The descendants of Canaan came to dwell in the region known as Palestine and Israel today. The Canaanites settled there along with their cousins the Amorites and Jebusites well before Abraham, circa 2500 BC. Among the archaeological sites of ancient Canaan which have been found are: Hazor, Megiddo, Beth Shan, Jericho, and Lachish. The northern Canaanites used a particular cuneiform script, built many walled cities ruled by kings as a city state, and were very civilized. Their civilization ended with the conquest of Joshua, but many of their cultures and religion, with its idols, remained with negative impact upon God's people.

Their religion featured many gods or idols among whom the male (Baal) and the female (Asherah) were repeatedly mentioned in the Old Testament. Their religion was lewd and base and included human sacrifice. Supposedly, their highest god was El who stayed in the background and conferred power to his offspring above. The remaining Canaanites in the land after Joshua's conquest led many of the Israelites to sin by worshiping in these idolatrous ways. In Joshua 24:23 Joshua saw this wickedness and declared, "Put away the foreign gods which are among you and incline your heart to the Lord God of Israel" (Nelson's *New Illustrated Bible Dictionary*, Thomas Nelson, Nashville, 1995, pp. 242-244).

By Faith Rahab Did Not Perish (Josh. 2:1-13; 6:22-25; Matt. 1:5)

In Hebrews 11:31, we read, "By faith **Rahab** the harlot did not perish along with those who were disobedient after she welcomed the spies in peace." The king of Jericho sent word to **Rahab**, "Bring out the men who have come to you, who have entered your house, for they have come to search out all the land." **Rahab**, who was a Canaanite harlot, had hidden the men and said that the men had gone out, and she did not know where they had gone. However, she had previously brought them up to the roof. She said to the men as recorded in Joshua 2:9-11, "I know that the Lord has given you the land, and that the terror of you has fallen on us, and that all the inhabitants of the land have melted away before you. For we heard how the Lord dried up the water of the Red Sea before you when you came out of Egypt, and what you did to the two kings of the Amorites who were beyond the Jordan, to Sihon and Og, whom you utterly destroyed. And when we heard it, our hearts melted and no courage remained in any man any longer because of you;

for the Lord your God, He is God in heaven above and on earth beneath." Oh that the Israelites of Jesus's time would have similarly recognized the power of God in the miracles done before them!

Rahab got the men to swear that she and her family would be spared. We know from Joshua that **Rahab** was spared and in fact became married to **Salmon** (Ruth 4:20; Matt. 1:4-5), one of the Israelites, and thus was in the lineage of Christ. Besides being mentioned in Hebrews 11:31, James in his epistle 2:25 says **Rahab** was justified by her works.

Questions

1. Describe Joshua's role under Moses. _____

_____

2. What was the report of the spies sent into the Promised Land? _____

_____

3. What was the punishment for not obeying God and not invading the Promised Land? _____

_____

4. How did God reveal His approval of Joshua to the Israelites?_____

_____

5. Paraphrase Joshua's farewell speech in chapter 24. _____

_____

_____

6. What did Rahab do to please God? _____

_____

7. Besides being spared, what other fact shows that Rahab was approved of God? _____

_____

8. What can we say about the destruction of Jericho that was discussed in Hebrews 11?_____

_____

9. What did God do for Joshua that exalted him in the eyes of all Israel (see Josh. 4:14-24)?_____

_____

10. Did Moses and Joshua have a lasting influence on the faithfulness of the Israelites? Explain. _____

_____

_____

11. Name some of the Canaanite tribes and from whom they descended._____

_____

Assignment for Lesson 9

Read Judges 1-21.

9 The Judges
Judges 1-21

Timeline: 1380-1043 BC. Revival of Hittite Empire; Pharaoh Ikhnaton develops a monotheistic religion; Tutankhamen of Egypt reinstates earlier gods (1341 BC); Ramses II (1300 BC) and Ramses III (1200 BC); Mythical Trojan War and the Trojan Horse (1300-1200 BC); Egypt and Assyria struggle for world power with Canaan as the battleground.

Points to Remember: Gideon, Barak, Samson, and Jephthah are the Judges singled out in Hebrews 11 for special recognition. Israel was attacked by various enemies and God sent judges to fight for and deliver them. The temptations from the Canaanite culture and idolatry influenced the children of Israel to sin again and again. Every man did what he thought was right in his own eyes (this is known as "situation ethics" today).

The Judges

After Joshua died, "there arose another generation who did not know the Lord . . . and they forsook the Lord and followed other gods. . . . Nevertheless, the Lord raised up judges who delivered them out of the hand of those who plundered them" (Judg. 2:10-16). When was the period of the judges? The subject has been debated so much that many do not try to give a date. However, there are some clues. The Exodus was about forty years before the Israelites were allowed to enter the Promised Land. We know that Joshua was born in Egypt and died at the age of 110. If we start with the death of Joshua and go through the rule of Samuel, then the period of the judges started about 1380 BC and ended about 1043 BC. Secular history records this period as having started around 1200 BC, but we know that Othniel (1374 BC) was Caleb's nephew and son-in-law, and it appears impossible that it was over 180 years till he became the first judge. Israel soon began to sin and serve the gods of the Canaanites. So, the Lord would punish the Israelites by using their enemies; then He would raise up judges who delivered the tribes affected by the persecution. Most of the judges only commanded a portion of Israel. After a judge died, the Israelites quickly turned away from God again into idolatry. This scenario was repeated over and over.

In Judges 3:1-3, we read, "Now these are the nations which the Lord left, to test Israel by them (that is), all who had not experienced any of the wars of Canaan; only in order that the generations of the sons of Israel might be taught war. . . . These nations are: the five lords of the Philistines . . . all the Canaanites and the Sardonians and the Hivites who lived in Mount Lebanon . . . they were for testing Israel, to find out if they would obey the commandments of the Lord." In Judges 21:25 we read, "In those days there was no king in Israel; everyone did what was right in his own eyes." One can see from reading Judges what "situation ethics" brought upon this nation and what it will bring upon any nation that does not believe and follow God's laws.

The first judge was Othniel (1374 BC) who delivered Israel from Cushan-risthathaim of Mesopotamia. Scholars have not as yet found this person in the secular history of Mesopotamia. This lesson will not focus upon all the judges, just the ones mentioned as being heroes of faith.

Hebrews 11 mentions four specific men among the faithful, so we will concentrate on them. Barak, Gideon, Jephthah, and Samson were named in Hebrews 11 as the ones who had the faith in God to defeat great armies with His help, although some had personal character flaws themselves.

Deborah and Barak (Judg. 4:1-5:31)

Deborah was a judge. She enlisted Barak to lead the fight against Jabin. However, Barak is the one who is named in Hebrews 11. These two will be discussed together as that was how they functioned in Judges four. "Then the sons of Israel did evil in the sight of the Lord . . . and the Lord sold them into the hand of Jabin the king of Canaan who reigned in Hazor; and the commander of his army was Sisera" (Judg. 4:1-4). This Jabin evidently was not the same man that Joshua defeated in his conquest of Canaan (Josh. 11:1). The Israelites cried unto the Lord, and He rose up Deborah with her military leader Barak. In Judges 4:4-6 we read, "Now Deborah, a prophetess was judging Israel at that time . . . and she sent and summoned Barak . . . 'take with you ten thousand men from the sons of Naphtali and from the sons of Zebulun and I will draw out Sisera (the commander of the troops of King Jabin) and his . . . chariots and his many troops . . . and I will give him into your hand.' Then Barak said to her, 'If you will go with me then I will go.' And she said, 'I will surely go with you; nevertheless, the honor shall not be yours . . . for the Lord will sell Sisera into the hands of a woman.'" We find as we read further in Judges 4 that evidently Barak was hesitant to tackle the large army of Sisera without the aid and comfort of the prophetess, Deborah. However, according to the song of Deborah, in Judges 5, the Lord caused a great rain to make the ground muddy, thus bogging down the chariots, giving Barak a great victory over the army. However, Sisera got down out of his chariot and escaped on foot to the tent of Jael, the wife of Heber the Kenite, for there was peace between Heber and King Jabin. Jael gave Sisera some milk; and while he was asleep, she took a tent peg and drove it into his temple so that he died. Thus, Jael got the glory for killing Sisera instead of Barak, as Deborah had prophesied.

Who was this Heber, the Kenite? In Numbers 10:29-32 we find that Heber's father, Hobab, was the son of Reuel the Midianite, Moses's father-in-law. Heber evidently went with his father, Hobab, as Moses asked, into the Promised Land and settled near Kedesh in Naphtali. Since Heber went with Moses into the Promised Land with the Israelites, he possibly became a proselyte and evidently married an Israelite named Jael.

Gideon (Judg. 6:1-8:35)

In Judges 6 through 8, we read of Gideon from the tribe of Manasseh. The Israelites had sinned again, and God had given them into the hands of Midian. Abraham had a son named Midian by his second wife Keturah. Midian's descendants came to live in northwest Arabia. When Moses fled from the Egyptians, he lived in Midian for 40 years and took a wife there named Zipporah. She was the daughter of a priest named Reuel (Jethro). Although, Moses had found them to be a friendly people, they later became the enemies of Israel. When the sons of Israel cried to the Lord on account of Midian, the Lord sent a prophet to them. In Judges 6:11 we read, "Then the angel of the Lord came and sat under the oak that was in Ophrah, which belonged to Joash the Abiezrite as his son Gideon was beating out wheat in the wine press in order to save it from the Midianites." If one consults a map, he will find that Ophrah was just south of Shechem in Manasseh. In Judges 6:12-16 Gideon was told by an angel of the Lord, "the Lord is with you, O valiant warrior." Gideon had doubts, as can be seen in Judges 6:13, "O my lord, if the Lord is with us, why then has all this happened to us? . . . the Lord has abandoned us and given us into the hand of Midian." Then the Lord God looked at him and said, "Go in this your strength and deliver Israel . . . I have sent you." But Gideon was meek and suggested he was neither valiant nor a warrior, that his family was the least in Manasseh, and that he was the youngest in his father's house. Gideon needed a sign to convince him that God was with him. Gideon offered a sacrifice to the Lord. As a sign, the angel touched the meat and the unleavened bread and fire sprang up from the rock and consumed them. Then the angel vanished. Gideon then realized he had seen an angel and was afraid. The Lord God said, "Peace to you, do not fear; you shall not die." That same night the Lord told him to pull down his father's altar of Baal, cut down the Asherah beside it, and build an altar and offer a bull upon it. The Baal was the male idol of the Canaanites, and the Asherah was the female goddess which was mostly represented as a wooden pillar.

Gideon, as God had told him, proceeded at night to pull down his father's altar of Baal so that his father's household and the men of the city would not see him. The next morning the men of the city saw that the Baal had been torn down and that another altar had been made; and they cried out, "Who did this thing?" It was discovered that it was Gideon, and a cry to have him killed was heard. But Joash, Gideon's father said, "Will you contend for Baal, or will you deliver him?" On that day Joash named Gideon "Jerubbaal," that is, "Let Baal contend against him."

The Lord decided to use Gideon to rid the Israelites of their oppressor Midian. Then the Spirit of the Lord came upon Gideon who blew his horn to summon all his kinsmen, the Abiezrites (offspring of Abiezer). He also sent messengers to Asher, Zebulun, and Naphtali, bringing his army to about 32,000 men. The Lord encouraged Gideon by the miracle of the dew and the fleece. The Lord told Gideon that the army was too large and that the fearful and trembling should return home. Twenty-two thousand returned. The Lord said that the people were still too many and that those who lapped water as they drank would be chosen. Only 300 men were left, a number that pleased the Lord, who then charged Gideon to go to the

camp of the Midianites. In case Gideon feared to go up against the Midianites, the Lord told him to take Purah, his servant, and sneak into the camp. Gideon overheard there a dream about a loaf of barley bread tumbling into the Midianite camp, overturning a tent. This dream was recognized by the Midianites as a warning from God and as victory for the "sword of Gideon."

Gideon did as the Lord commanded; and his men cried, "A sword for the Lord and for Gideon." God caused great confusion among the Midianites, and they even used their swords against themselves, giving the Lord and Gideon a great victory. Think what great faith Gideon, a lowly son of a lowly family, had in the Lord that enabled him to lead 300 men into battle against an army too large to number. Truly, Gideon was a hero of faith. The men wanted to make Gideon a king after this victory; but Gideon said, "I will not rule over you, nor shall my son rule over you; the Lord shall rule over you." Nevertheless, Gideon later set up a golden ephod in Ophrah. It became a snare to Gideon and to the Israelites because the people began to worship it.

Jephthah

In Judges 10:18-12:7, one can read about Jephthah. The leaders of Gilead were being oppressed by Ammon. Ben-Ammi, as students of the Old Testament will remember, was a son of Lot. His descendants settled east of the Jordan River and founded the Country of Ammon, which

was south of the area of Gilead and Gideon's tribe of Manasseh. Although distant cousins of the Israelites, the Ammonites became their enemy. The leaders of Israel said, "Who is the man who will begin to fight against the sons of Ammon? He shall become head over all the inhabitants of Gilead." In chapter 11, Jephthah was presented as a valiant warrior; but he was the son of a harlot from Gilead. He had been driven out of his father's house and told he would not inherit. Jephthah fled to the land of Tob and gathered a rough band of followers. The leaders of Gilead summoned Jephthah to lead them, but Jephthah replied, "Did you not hate me and drive me from my father's house? So why have you come to me now when you are in trouble?" Nevertheless, Jephthah agreed to lead them if they would make him head over them. Jephthah, unlike Gideon, wanted to be the leader of his people against the Ammonites.

The Spirit of the Lord came upon Jephthah. He made the infamous vow that, if the Lord would give Ammon into his hands, then whatever came out of the doors of his house to meet him on his return should be the Lord's and be offered as a burnt offering. Jephthah subdued the Ammonites with the sword, and unfortunately his only child and daughter came out to greet him. Although he regretted making the vow, he said, "I have given my word to the Lord, and I cannot take it back." His daughter had to remain a virgin, and she

"Men of Whom the World Was Not Worthy"

dedicated her life to God. (Some think she was also sacrificed; but since human sacrifice was forbidden by God, this author believes that part of the vow was not carried out.)

Jephthah judged Israel six years and died. One may wonder why Jephthah was singled out as one of the judges to be honored as a faithful hero. Perhaps it was because not only did he show his faith to God in believing he could defeat Ammon, but his faithfulness was also demonstrated in keeping his vow to God.

Samson

Perhaps there is no judge better known than Samson, the last judge we will study. He is known to all as not only the strongest man to have lived, but a man of weak moral character. One might question why Samson was included in the list of the heroes of faith, but perhaps the phrase in Hebrews 11:34 explains the choice, "who by faith . . . from weakness was made strong." Samson had been dedicated to God as a Nazirite in childhood, and God foretold to his mother that he would deliver Israel from the hands of the Philistines. The Philistines had troubled the Israelites for years. Living on the coast of the Mediterranean Sea, the Philistines were a crude, seafaring, and warrior peoples. They possessed an early ability to make superior metal weapons and thus dominated the nations around them.

Did God know that Samson would have weaknesses that would do him harm? I believe that He did, but God also knew He could use this impetuous man to do His bidding and punish the Philistines for their oppression of the Israelites. In Judges 15:11-17 we find how well Samson, with God's help, could fight when he killed a thousand of his enemies with only the jawbone of a donkey.

Samson's infatuation with Delilah, a beautiful daughter of the Philistines, eventually caused him to give up the secret to his strength. Without that strength, Samson was blinded and imprisoned by his mortal enemy, the Philistines. It was while in this humbled position that Samson's faith became the strongest. In Judges 16, Samson offered this prayer to God, "O Lord God, please remember me and strengthen me just this time, O God, that I may at once be avenged of the Philistines for my two eyes. . . .Let me die with the Philistines." Samson grasped the two middle pillars in the temple of Dagon, the god of the Philistines, and tore down the pillars so that the temple fell; and Samson killed more in his death than he did in his life. Thus, he had judged Israel 20 years. One mourns because of what Samson's life of moral weakness had caused, but rejoices that in the end his faith returned. His prayer to God gave him the strength which allowed him to carry out God's purpose.

Do not forget a very valuable lesson from the time of the judges. In Judges 21:25 one reads, "In those days there was no king in Israel; everyone did what was right in his own eyes." This was clearly "Situation Ethics." One can plainly see what problems will result from adhering to this philosophy, both to individuals and also to nations.

Questions

1. Who was the first judge over Israel? _____

2. What judges are mentioned by name in Hebrews 11?_____

_____

3. Should one consider that the other judges raised up by God were not worthy? _____

4. Discuss Judges 21:25 in light of present day philosophies of "Humanism" and "Situation Ethics." _____

_____

_____

5. What are the strong and weak traits of Gideon? _____

_____

6. Who was the enemy that Gideon defeated with God's help? _____

7. What were the two main gods of the idolatrous people of Canaan? _____

8. What was the size of Gideon's army? Of Midian's army? _____

_____

9. Discuss the "Sword of Gideon." _____

_____

10. Tell the story of Barak and Deborah, and who they defeated. _____

_____

11. Who were the enemies of the Israelites whom Jephthah fought? _____

12. What vow did Jephthah make to God? _____

_____

13 In what vow was Samson brought up? _____

14. Who was Samson and Israel's enemy at the time? _____

15. Discuss how God used Samson's weaknesses and strengths for His purpose. _____

_____

_____

Assignment for Lesson 10

Read 1 Samuel 1:1-28:3.

"Men of Whom the World Was Not Worthy"

Samuel

1 Samuel 1:1-28:3

10

Timeline: circa 1080 BC

Points to Remember: Elkanah was of the tribe of Ephraim and had two wives, Hannah and Pininnah. Hannah was barren and prayed to the Lord that, if He would grant her a male child, she would dedicate the child to the Lord all of his life as a Nazirite. Her son, Samuel, grew to become a judge and a prophet.

Samuel

Hannah was pouring out her soul to the Lord; and Eli the priest said, "May the God of Israel grant your petition of Him." The Lord did indeed grant her petition, and Samuel was born. The name Samuel means "someone from God." Hannah waited until Samuel was weaned and brought him to Eli to raise so that he could learn how to minister to the Lord. Samuel obeyed Eli and ministered to the Lord. Later, when the Lord called Samuel in the middle of the night, he answered, "Speak for thy servant is listening," and the Lord spoke to him.

Eli had two sons, Hophni and Phinehas, who were worthless and did not serve the Lord. Neither did Eli restrain them. Because of these things, a man of God told Eli that both of his sons would die on the same day and his family would not have an old man forever (1 Sam. 2:31-33). Eli's descendants would not be the chief priests.

Samuel was then told by the Lord what He was going to do to Eli and his sons. Samuel grew, and the Lord was with him, and "let none of His words fail" (fall to the ground). All Israel from Dan even to Beersheba knew that Samuel was confirmed as a prophet of the Lord.

In 1 Samuel 4, we read of the defeat by the Philistines. The Israelites were attacked by their enemy, Philistia. Without consulting God, the Israelites brought the Ark of the Covenant into battle. Without God to help the Israelites, the Philistines killed 30,000 and captured the Ark. Upon hearing of the death of his two sons and the capture of the Ark, Eli fell over backwards and died. Thus, the words of the Lord came true.

Now unfolds a remarkable account of what happens to the Philistines who took the Ark to Ashdod, one of their principle cities, and placed it in the temple of Dagon, their god. The idolatrous statue of Dagon fell over and was destroyed. God shortly sent tumors to afflict the inhabitants of Ashdod.

The people recognized that their affliction was because of the Ark and send it to Gath and to Ekron where the same tumors arose. Also, mice were sent by the Lord to invade the country as long as the Ark was in Philistia. (Philistia will

be studied further in the discussion about David.)

The Ark became very odious to the Philistines and was sent back to Israel on a cart pulled along by cows separated from their young. If the cows pulling the Ark went straight to Israel, this would be a sign that God accepted the Ark. The Philistines also sent a guilt offering of five golden tumors and five golden mice. The "tumors" suggested that the Philistines were suffering from buboes that came from a plague spread by mice. Was this bubonic plague? God did accept the offering, and the Philistines were cured. The Israelites, not knowing the law, looked into the Ark upon its return. The Lord struck down 50,700 men because they looked into the Ark.

What was in the Ark? It held the tablets containing the Ten Commandments, an omer of manna in a golden jar, and Aaron's rod that budded (Heb. 9:4).

After the disaster above, Samuel spoke to the people saying, "If you return to the Lord with all your heart, remove the foreign gods . . . and direct your hearts to the Lord . . . . He will deliver you from the hand of the Philistines." The Lord delivered the Israelites (after they had repented) by routing the Philistines with thunder. Samuel set up a large stone in memory of God's victory. Samuel named that stone "Ebenezer," saying, "Hither hath the Lord helped us." "Ebenezer" means "stone of help." The song "O Thou Fount of Every Blessing," in many song books, commemorates this episode. Figuratively, how can one raise his or her Ebenezer?

"And it came to pass when Samuel was old that he appointed his sons judges over Israel. Then the elders of Israel gathered together and came to Samuel and said to him . . . 'your sons do not walk in your ways, now make us a king to judge us like all the nations.' And the Lord said to Samuel, 'Listen to the voice of the people for they have not rejected you, but they have rejected Me from being king over them'" (1 Sam. 8:1-9).

Samuel warned them of the customs of kings who would take taxes and make their children work for them, but they would not listen. Then God directed Samuel to anoint Saul king over Israel. After Saul had been king for several years, he disobeyed the Lord by not destroying all of the Amalekites and their oxen and sheep as God had commanded him. Saul argued that he did obey the Lord's command, only he actually did not because he brought back Agag the king. Samuel said, "What then is this bleating of the sheep in my ears, and the lowing of the oxen which I hear?" Saul said the people took some of the spoil to sacrifice to the Lord; but Samuel said, "Behold, to obey is better than sacrifice, and to heed than the fat of rams. For rebellion is as the sin of divination. Because you have rejected the word of the Lord, He has also rejected you from being king" (1 Sam. 15:13-26).

In 1 Samuel 16, Samuel was directed by God to anoint David as the next king of Israel. As Samuel poured the oil on his head, the Spirit of the Lord came mightily upon David and departed from Saul. David, who is also a hero of faith, will be studied in the next lesson.

Samuel led a wonderful life for the Lord as a judge and a prophet, and was revered by all Israel. One can read in 1 Samuel 25:1, "Then Samuel died; and all Israel gathered together and mourned for him, and buried him at his house in Ramah." Truly he was a "hero of faith."

Questions

1. How did Samuel come to be dedicated to the Lord? _____

_____

2. Who was Eli? _____What were his sons' names? _____

3. What was the significance of the five golden tumors and the five golden mice? _____

_____

4. How did the Israelites break the law concerning the Ark and what consequences ensued? _____

_____

5. What is an Ebenezer, and how can we raise one today? _____

_____

6. Why did the Israelites sin by wanting a king? Is this a lesson for us today? _____

_____

7. In chapter 12, what did Samuel ask of the people? _____

_____

8. What was King Saul's sin in 1 Samuel 15? _____

9. "To _____ is better than _____."

Assignment for Lesson 11

Read 1 Samuel 16-1 Kings 2.

"Men of Whom the World Was Not Worthy"

David

1 Samuel 16–1 Kings 2

11

Timeline 1041-971 BC: Assyria rising to power; Phoenicians developed supremacy in the eastern Mediterranean and created an alphabet that is the basis of the modern English alphabet; Etruscans arrived in Italy; Queen of Sheba.

Points to Remember: In 1 Samuel 13:14 and Acts 13:22 God said, "I have found **David** the son of Jesse, a man after My own heart, who will do all My will." **David's** faith in God was strong enough to stand against Goliath and all of God's enemies. David's sins with Bathsheba and against Uriah were forgiven because of his great and true repentance. Although **David** suffered the consequences of his sins, he was allowed to continue to rule Israel, and be in the lineage of Christ.

David

David is not discussed in detail in Hebrews 11, but is mentioned as one of the faithful heroes. And because **David** is the greatest of the three kings of the United Kingdom, his life and the historical world events that affected him will be studied together. **Solomon**, his son, was allowed to build the temple; and the date of that project is the first date in the Bible that is confirmed by secular history. From that date, which was 966 BC, one can date **David's** rule with some certainty as 1011-971 BC.

We know that **David** is called "a man after God's own heart," and his many Psalms give us a rare insight into his character. In 1 Samuel 16 we find that God told Samuel to anoint a son of **Jesse** to be the next king. Samuel thought it might be Eliab because of his height and bearing; but God said, "Do not look at his appearance or at the height of his stature for God sees not as man sees, for man looks at the outward appearance, but the Lord looks at the heart." After looking at all the sons of **Jesse**, **David** was brought before Samuel. "And the Lord said, 'Arise, anoint him; for this is he.'" In 1 Samuel 16:13 we find that the Spirit of the Lord came mightily upon **David** from that day forward.

David is later called by his father to take food to three of his brothers who have gone with King Saul to face the Philistines. The Philistines had a champion, a giant named Goliath who was nine and a half feet tall, who challenged the Israelites to find a man to fight him. All Bible believers should know the outcome. In one of his greatest showings of faith, young **David** takes up the challenge and kills Goliath with only his slingshot. For he said, "The Lord who delivered me from the paw of the lion and the paw of the bear, He will deliver me from the hand of the Philistine." In 1 Samuel 17 one reads that **David** said to Goliath, who cursed him, "I come in the name of the Lord of hosts, the God of the armies of Israel, whom you have taunted. This day the Lord will deliver you into my hands, and I will strike you down and remove your head . . . that all the earth may know that there is a God in Israel."

In 1 Samuel 18 one can read that many were beginning to praise **David** above the reigning King Saul; they said, "Saul has slain his thousands, and David his ten thousands." Saul's jealousy of **David** defined the rest of his reign. When he heard that, Saul became very angry and said, "What more can he have than the kingdom." From that time, Saul sought to kill **David**. **David** was afraid for his life, but he did not lift a finger against Saul because Saul was still God's anointed. The Lord was with **David**, and he prospered in spite of Saul's persecution. **David** wrote Psalm 57 when he was hiding from Saul in a cave. It should be read to get a true feeling of how much faith and trust **David** had in the Lord to save him.

David never ceased to inquire of the Lord what to do in trying circumstances. At times, he even sent for an ephod (a garment worn by the high priest) to aid in his prayers.

David finally got his appointment to reign as king when Saul and his son, Jonathan, were killed fighting the Philistines. Unfortunately, Abner, who had been the commander of Saul's army, got Ishbosheth seated to reign over Gilead, Ephraim, and Benjamin. This circumstance left **David's** rule limited to Judah. There was a war between the house of Saul and the house of **David** for two years. **David** grew stronger, and the house of Saul grew weaker.

After reigning for two years, Ishbosheth and his general, Abner, were killed and mourned by **David**. **David** was crowned king of all Israel and reigned from Hebron for a total of seven years. Later, **David** with God's help attacked Jebus (later called Jerusalem) and moved his seat of power and reigned there for 33 years.

We have seen the faith of **David**, but now in Jerusalem one begins to see his weaknesses. When the Philistines heard that **David** had been crowned king, they came to fight. **David** sought the guidance of the Lord. The Lord gave the Philistines into **David's** hand, but then **David** moved the Ark of the Covenant toward Jerusalem without consulting the Scriptures. As a result, Uzzah died trying to keep the Ark from falling off an ox cart. Although one feels sympathy for Uzzah for trying to do the right thing by saving the Ark, the Lord teaches us here by example that one is not allowed to do what he thinks is right, but what God commands. **David** later brought the Ark as well as great sacrifices to God. This time the Ark was carried correctly by the priests, safely to Jerusalem.

David's most famous sin occurred when he desired Bathsheba, lay with her, and had her husband Uriah killed in battle. When confronted by his sin, **David** confessed his sin to the Lord and wept and prayed. Although **David** confessed his sin, humbled himself before the Lord, and was forgiven, he nevertheless suffered the consequences of that sin and lost the firstborn son of Bathsheba. The Lord said that the sword would never depart from his house; nevertheless, the Lord loved **Solomon**, the next son born to Bathsheba. Enemies of Israel would fight Israel and **David** for the rest of his life; and **David** would have his throne challenged by two of his sons, Absalom and Adonijah.

At the end of his life, **David** was very old and made **Solomon** king and charged him to continue in the ways of the Lord. Despite the great sin that **David** did, God singled him out as a "man after My own heart." Most of the time, **David** put God first in his life and studied God's law with reverence. With such great faith that he could face and kill the giant, Goliath; it is not surprising the author of Hebrews, by inspiration, included **David** as a Hero of Faith.

The Philistines

The Philistines were one of the enemies and countries that affected **David** and Israel. Most of the other surrounding countries were introduced earlier such as Moab, Ammon, and the Canaanites. Since the Philistines were the most prominent peoples that **David** dealt with, they will be studied now.

The country of the Philistines was approximately the area known as the Gaza Strip today. In fact, Gaza was one of the Philistine cities. Pottery remains in the principle cities such as Gaza, Ashkelon, and Ashdod provided the first archeological evidence of the Philistine presence in Palestine. It is said that the word "Palestine" itself comes from the word for Philistine. Secular history and biblical history depart as to the time of the origin of the Philistines, for in Genesis, **Abraham** and **Isaac** are shown to have dealings with two Abimelechs (kings of Philistia). Thus, the Bible gives a much earlier date for the migration of the Philistines into Canaan. In Genesis 10:6-14 one reads, "and the sons of Ham were . . . Mizraim the father of . . . Cashluhim (or Caphtorim) from which came the Philistines." In Amos 9:7, Caphtor is mentioned as being the original home of the Philistines and is widely believed to be the island of Crete. It is interesting that the Septuagint version reads "Cappadocia" instead of "Caphtor." Perhaps the Philistine peoples were at some time in Cappadocia.

Some secular historians say the Sea Peoples were the Philistines and intended to settle in or near Egypt, but were repulsed by Ramses III and settled in Canaan. Since their origin was thought even by these "scholars" to be from Crete and the Aegean area, they have been referred to as Greeks by some. These "Sea Peoples" who invaded the coast of Canaan around 1180-1150 BC were thought to have founded the five city states of Gath, Gaza, Ashkelon, Ashdod, and Ekron. There may have been two migrations of Philistines. The biblical account which reveals the Philistines were descended from Mizraim will be relied upon in this study.

The seafaring skills of the Philistines also probably made for good trade with countries like Phoenicia. They brought with them Aegean style pottery, architecture, and political culture; however, they quickly adapted to the Canaanite language and culture. The primary idolatrous god of the Philistines was Dagon whose temple Samson destroyed at his death. The Philistines were finally subdued by Tiglath-Pileser III of Assyria in his conquest of Israel around 722 BC and later absorbed by the Babylonians into their Empire.

Samuel, Saul, and **David** all had clashes with the Philistines who had long held a monopoly on iron-smithing and thus had more superior weapons than the Israelites. Because of this monopoly, the Philistines were able to exert control over the Israelites for many years. The description of Goliath's armor is consistent with this knowledge. The Philistines were a rough and immoral people, and calling a person a "Philistine" is still a very derogatory description. Although the Philistines continued to exist after the time of **David**, they were never again the threat to Israel as they previously had been.

Questions

1. What were **David's** greatest accomplishments? _____

_____

2. What were **David's** weaknesses? _____

_____

3. Even though he was forgiven, what were the consequences of **David's** sins to himself and to Israel?

_____

4. What does the fact that **David** and **Bathsheba's** son, **Solomon,** was chosen to be the king of Israel and in the lineage of Christ with God's blessing teach us? _____

_____

5. How was **David** a man after God's own heart? _____

_____

6. Discuss glimpses of **David's** character as revealed in his Psalms. _____

_____

7. When **David** faced Goliath and his other enemies, how did he give God the glory? _____

_____

8. What was **David's** shortcoming in his attempt to move the Ark to Jerusalem? _____

_____

9. Discuss the origin and attributes of the Philistines. _____

_____

_____

POSTSCRIPT

This author hopes that these lessons have proved useful in the study of the Old Testament Heroes. The historical and contemporary events have been included in an effort to make this study interesting and informative, as well as to give a perspective of what life was like during this period of the "Heroes of Faith."

Rand Zuber, M.D.

"Men of Whom the World Was Not Worthy"